Praise for *Feminism: Transmissions and Retransmissions*

"Anthropologist Marta Lamas's book is a compelling examination of a variety of theoretical debates among contemporary feminists around the globe. From her location as a scholar/activist within the women's movement in Mexico, she charts the evolution of her own intellectual/political journey over the past three decades. This text is a model for feminist theorists who are committed to similar self-reflections about a movement that has helped to transform both the academy and civil society."

—Beverly Guy-Sheftall, Founding Director, Women's Research and Resource Center,
Anna Julia Cooper Professor of Women's Studies, Spelman College,
and past president of the National Women's Studies Association

"Marta Lamas is a refreshing, incisive voice and the history she charts is a welcome and informative one. The English translation of *Feminism* poses questions and problems that remain points of contention in feminist work across institutions and social spaces. This will be a timely and useful resource for students and scholars interested in learning more about theoretical and political tensions that shaped late twentieth-century Mexican feminism."

—Rosemary Hennessy, Director, Center for the Study of Women,
Gender, and Sexuality and Professor, Department of English, Rice University

"Three main scholarly heritages—anthropology, feminism, and Marxism—overlap and inspire Lamas's approach in this veritable tour de force. This book takes up from the early days of women's consciousness-raising, to today's global feminist commitment, to human rights and a democratic praxis founded on inclusionary politics. A feminist in the trenches since the 1970s, Lamas offers new generations of students and scholars a highly accessible text that will persist, undoubtedly, as a required reference for years to come. This is a book you want to read, teach, and keep at hand."

—Norma Klahn, Professor of Literature, University of California, Santa Cruz

"Lamas gives us new forms of feminist theory and politics from the perspective of her own long-standing engagement with Mexican feminism. Here, we learn how terms like 'feminism,' 'gender,' 'sexual difference,' and 'essentialism' have been historically and locally inflected by *mujerismo*, sectarian discord, and Zapatista feminism, as well as by common struggles against the Catholic Church, the machismo of workers' parties, *indigenismo* movements on the left, and habits of political corruption that have encouraged rape and abuse. A profound reflection on the place of 'theory' in future iterations of feminist theory and political activism rounds out the work's compass. Lamas's groundbreaking book, like others in this important series, reminds us that theory is not a eurocentric affair, but rather a multisited thinking in and of the world."

—Emily Apter, Professor of French and Comparative Literature,
New York University and series editor of *Translation/Transnation*

"Marta Lamas is an extraordinary thinker and writer. Her work is pathbreaking and original. This book will bring her and the history of Mexican feminism to a broad audience. As theory and history it is an indispensable read."

—Joan W. Scott, Harold F. Linder Professor of Social Science,
Institute for Advanced Study

"Lamas's essays span three decades of intellectual and political leadership in Mexico's feminist movement. Among the challenges they throw down, two stand out: politics will go nowhere without theory, and feminism must overcome dogmatism and 'arrogant' sectarianism if it is to develop a viable political base. The *Theory in the World* series is an ideal setting for the transmission of Lamas's work."

—Mary Louise Pratt, Professor, Department of Spanish and
Portuguese Languages and Literatures, New York University

THEORY IN THE WORLD

Edited by Gayatri Chakravorty Spivak and Hosam Aboul-Ela

Published by Palgrave Macmillan:

Feminism: Transmissions and Retransmissions
By Marta Lamas, translated by John Pluecker with an Introduction by Jean Franco

Between Conformity and Resistance: Essays on Politics, Culture, and the State
By Marilena Chauí, translated and edited by Maite Conde

Neighborhood and Boulevard: Reading the Modern Arab City (forthcoming)
By Khaled Ziadeh, translated by Samah Selim

Feminism

Transmissions and Retransmissions

Marta Lamas

Translated by John Pluecker
Introduction by Jean Franco

palgrave
macmillan

FEMINISM
Copyright © Marta Lamas, 2011.

All rights reserved.

First published in 2011 by
PALGRAVE MACMILLAN®
in the United States—a division of St. Martin's Press LLC,
175 Fifth Avenue, New York, NY 10010.

Where this book is distributed in the UK, Europe and the rest of the world,
this is by Palgrave Macmillan, a division of Macmillan Publishers Limited,
registered in England, company number 785998, of Houndmills,
Basingstoke, Hampshire RG21 6XS.

Palgrave Macmillan is the global academic imprint of the above companies
and has companies and representatives throughout the world.

Palgrave® and Macmillan® are registered trademarks in the United States,
the United Kingdom, Europe and other countries.

ISBN: 978-0-230-10508-9

Library of Congress Cataloging-in-Publication Data

Lamas, Marta.
    [Feminismo. English]
    : Feminism : transmissions and retransmissions / Marta Lamas ;
  translated by John Pluecker ; introduction by Jean Franco.
      p. cm. – (Theory in the World)
    Includes bibliographical references and index.
    ISBN 978-0-230-10508-9 (hardback)
     1. Feminism. 2. Feminism—Mexico. 3. Women—Social conditions.
  I. Title. II. Series.

HQ1233.L3513 2011
305.420972—dc22   2010042328

A catalogue record of the book is available from the British Library.

Design by Newgen Imaging Systems (P) Ltd., Chennai, India.

First edition: May 2011

10 9 8 7 6 5 4 3 2 1

Transferred to Digital Printing in 2012

Contents

Theory in the World: A General Introduction

"Theory" is an English transcription of the Greek *theorein*. Corresponding words exist in the major European languages. Our series, "Theory in the World," works within these limits. "Theory" has been creolized into innumerable languages. Yet the phenomenon of "seeing or making visible correctly"— the meaning in Greek that will still suffice—does not necessarily relate to that word—"theory"—in those languages. That describes the task of the editors of a translated series of theory in the world.

Heidegger thinks that truth is destined to be thought by the man of "Western Europe."[1] Our series does not offer a legitimizing counteressentialism. Take a look at the map and see how tiny Europe is, not even really a continent, but, as Derrida would say, a *cap*, a headland.[2] Such a tiny place, yet who can deny Derrida's description, which is a historical and empirical observation? Look at the tables of contents of the most popular critical anthologies, and you will see corroboration of the essentialist conviction that goes with the historical claim. The counteressentialism is reflected in the choice of critics from "the rest of the world." Just being non-white is the counteressence.

The influential *Norton Anthology of Theory and Criticism*, for example, lets in only Maimonides before the modern university system kicks in.[3] But, even if they had let in Khaled Ziadeh, Marta Lamas, Marilena Chauí, and Arindam Chakrabarti, the material would be determined by the epistemological procedures of that system. Norton lets in W. E. B. Du Bois, the first African American to get a doctorate from Harvard, the man who felt that "of the greatest importance was the opportunity which my *Wanderjahre* [wandering years] in Europe gave of looking at the world as a man and not simply from a narrow racial and provincial outlook."[4] Then we get Zora Neale Hurston (Columbia), Langston Hughes (Harlem Renaissance via Columbia), Frantz Fanon (University of Lyons), Chinua Achebe (University College, Ibadan), Stuart Hall (Oxford), Ngũgĩ wa Thiong'o (Leeds), Taban Lo Liyong (Iowa), Henry Owuwor-Anyuumba (Iowa), Spivak (Cornell), Houston Baker (UCLA), Gloria Anzaldúa (UCSC), Homi Bhabha (Oxford), Barbara Christian (Columbia), Barbara Smith (Mount Holyoke), Henry Louis Gates, Jr. (Cambridge), bell hooks (UCSC). The point I am making is not that these wonderful writers have not challenged Eurocentrism. It is that they are sabotaging from within and this is a historical fact that must be turned around so that there is a chance for truth to reveal itself. Fanon stands out, not because he is not a university man, but because he is the only one who clearly operated outside the Euro-U.S., though he was what Du Bois would call a Black European, literally fighting Europe, also from within, located in a geographical exterior.

(In the next most influential anthology, the rest-of-the-world entries are almost identical, but for Audre Lorde [Columbia], Geraldine Heng [Cornell], Ania Loomba [Sussex], Chidi Oklonkwo [Georgia Tech], Jamaica Kincaid [Franconia and the New School]).[5] Again, Fanon is the only working "outsider." I am sure the general pattern is repeated everywhere. I have myself been so tokenized through my long career as representing "Third World criticism" that I am particularly alive to the problem.[6]

Yet our list is not really different. Marta Lamas teaches at the National Autonomous University in Mexico, founded in 1551; Khaled Ziadeh went to the Sorbonne, and Marilena Chauí is a Professor at the University of São Paulo. Lamas repeatedly assures us that affirmative action for gender justice works in the "developed countries," Chauí offers us Spinoza, and Ziadeh recommends modernity via an earlier imperial formation, the Ottomans. So what is the difference?

Our position is against a rest-of-the-world counteressentialism, which honors the history versus tradition binary opposition. We recognize that a hegemonic Euro-U.S. series can only access work abroad that is continuous with Euro-U.S. radicalism. To open ourselves to what lies beyond is another kind of effort. Within the limits of our cause, we focus, then, on another phenomenon.

The history of the past few centuries has produced patterns of bilateral resistance. The formation is typically my nation-state, my region, my cultural formation over against "the West." These days there are global efforts at conferences, events, and organizations that typically take the form of the Euro-U.S. at the center, and a whole collection of "other cultures," who connect through the imperial languages, protected by a combination of sanctioned ignorance and superficial solidarities, ignoring the internal problems when they are at these global functions.[7] The model is the fact and discipline of preservation. By the Nara document of 1994, Japan insisted that preservation should be not only of built space but also of intangible cultural heritage. What started was the model that I have described above. It is now a tremendous capital-intensive fact of our world.

In and through our series, we want to combat this tendency. We want not only to present texts from different national origins to the U.S. readership, but also to point out how each is singular in the philosophical sense, namely universalizable, though never universal. We are not working for area studies niche-marketing, though the work is always of specialist quality. In the interest of creating a diversified collectivity outside of the English readership, the editors plan to hold annual conferences, interactive on the Web.

The story begins for me in a conversation with the Subaltern Studies collective in 1986—asking them if I could arrange the publication of a selection—because they were not available in the United States. A long term preoccupation, then. To this was added Hosam Aboul-Ela's 2007 consolidation of a thought that was growing inside me: from the rest of the world literary editors wanted fiction, poetry, drama—raw material. Theory came generally from "us." When Palgrave Macmillan called on me, I called on Hosam to be my coeditor for this series.

In the intervening three decades a small difference had imposed itself. Earlier I had felt that my brief within the profession was to share and show the work overseas was really "theoretical" by Western sizing. (I use the word "size" here in the sense of *pointure* in Derrida.)[8] Hence "strategic use of essentialism." Now I also feel the reader must learn that "theory" need not look the same everywhere, that for the independent mind, too much training in producing the European model in stylistic detail might hamper. (From my teacher training work in rural India I understand that it is the illiterate man who understands things best because his considerable intelligence has not been hobbled by bad education or gender oppression. The lesson here is not that everyone should be illiterate, but that strong minds should not be ruined by bad education or imperatives to imitate.)

This caution applies to *Neighborhood and Boulevard* by Khaled Ziadeh—not bad education, obviously, but the imperative to imitate "French Theory." Ziadeh theorizes by space and repetition; Hosam Aboul-Ela's Introduction walks us through it. There are plenty of people writing in Arabic who produce work competitive with the best in European-style "theory." Reading Ziadeh, as Aboul-Ela points out, we have to learn to recognize "theory" in another guise. My own work profits from his account of the de-Ottomanization of the city by the French into an "Islamic" space; because I think de-Ottomanization, still active in our time, has a history as old as the Fall of Constantinople, and, reterritorialized, backward into Byzantium.

Our series has only just begun. I have described our goal with appropriate modesty: to translate theoretical material operating outside the Euro-U.S., not readily available to metropolitan readership but continuous with the episteme, even as "hybridity" keeps the local elsewhere. Yet there are also singular enclaves in many places where teaching and thinking apparently take place in less continuous epistemic formation. To acquire texts from these enclaves would require the kind of preparation, partly traditionalist, partly anthropologistic, that I do not possess. Perhaps, if our initial forays succeed, we will be able to fling our net wider: particularly important in the context of sub-Saharan Africa, where strong theoretical writing in the imperial languages (also languages of Africa, of course) flourishes and holds influence. For theoretical writing in the indigenous languages, not necessarily imitating the European model, contained within internal conflict, avoiding the anthropologist in the name of tradition will be on our agenda.

For now, I have arrived, after an initial meeting at the Modern Language Association, to an understanding of an activist "Task of the Editor," that I have outlined above: to combat the bilateralism: my place and your Euro-U.S., that legitimizes Eurocentrism by reversal.

We start our list with Marta Lamas, *Feminism: Transmissions and Retransmissions*. Lamas is a feminist who theorizes as she practices. Her work is full of singular Mexican specificities. My own work can build on hers. As Jean Franco writes in her Introduction: "Lamas remains required reading." I will spell out how Lamas and I relate. The human being and advanced primates are defined by the difference between what they need and what they can make. In this difference rise art, capital, the intuition of the transcendental, and human continuity as history. Each one of these is medicine and poison. This difference is theorized— and it is silly to think the primitive is incapable of theory—in terms of the only difference empirically available to us- sexual difference. It is this that Lamas calls "the invariable traits of biological difference." Gender (or "what we now call gender," Lamas again) is the grounding instrument of abstraction. I could go further, but for the series introduction, this is enough.

Next comes Khaled Ziadeh, of whom I have already written, and Marilena Chauí, *Between Conformity and Resistance: Essays on Politics, Culture, and the State*. Chauí's specificity is Brazil, as Étienne Balibar's is France, and Partha Chatterjee's India. Readership of English and French have had no difficulty in finding what is universalizable in the texts of these latter two. We hope that they will proceed in the same way with Chauí. In "Brazil's Foundational Myth" she speaks to India, Africa, Israel, and many other countries. Her discussions of citizenship and democracy have worldwide application. Her comments on the administered university is right on target for that phenomenon everywhere. Her discussion of popular religion has validity for discussions of secularism today. Her analysis of ethical philosophy, diagnosing "ethical ideology" as a do-gooding that presupposes victimhood and therefore evil, is applicable to the presuppositions of human rights and the international civil society. When she writes about Spinoza, it is an implicit critique of the digital idealism of Michael Hardt and Antonio Negri's recent work, which takes Spinozan categories such as "multitude," "singularity," and so on, and simply empiricizes them, ignoring that Spinoza was writing from within a position that could theorize only the righteous state. Again, there is much more material that I could cover, but I will stop here and let you enjoy the text for yourselves.

(I am sorry that she opposes a caricatured "postmodernism," especially since she herself is sometimes perceived as a "postmodern" writer.)[9]

Down the line, we are planning to bring forward proposals for translations of Luis Tapia, *History and Politics in the Work of René Zavaleta*, as well as a text by the "Bolivian Gramsci," René Zavaleta Mercado himself; *Deho, Geho, Bandhutto*, a text by Arindam Chakrabarti, and Nasr Hamid Abu Zayd, *Discourse and Interpretation*; we are negotiating for women's texts from China, Korea, and Japan.

Our translators share with us the problems of translation for each unique text, at least hinting to the reader that, although the activity of translating is altogether pleasurable, to accept translations passively as a substitute for the "original" closes doors. We will not give up the foolish hope that a careful translation, sharing problems, will lead to language-learning.

Read our series as a first step, then. Come to the annual conferences where all of the authors and translators will gather, to ask: what is it to theorize, in our world?

GAYATRI CHAKRAVORTY SPIVAK
Columbia University

Translator's Note

As Marta Lamas tells us in her preface, the essays included in this volume have been copied and circulated among feminist groups throughout Latin America who have shared, discussed, and debated them vigorously. The ideas in these essays draw from feminist theorists and scholars around the world as Lamas works to interpret and re-contextualize them in a Latin American context. In this way, these texts can be seen as already in and of themselves born out of a process of translation, in the general sense. Many of the dialogues, particularly around issues of gender and affirmative action, already cross boundaries of language and nation, as Lamas reads and relocates feminist thinking from Europe and the Americas. This preexisting translation made for its own set of challenges at the moment of translating Lamas's work into English, in the narrow sense. We can see these issues as Lamas redefines words used in other contexts and appropriates words from other languages, introducing subtle distinctions in meaning.

One example is found in the term *"mujerismo,"* which is fundamental to her arguments in favor of discussion and debate within the feminist movement, particularly in Latin America. Lamas uses this word to refer to an identitarian and essentialist branch of Mexican feminism that finds an almost mystical value in the core identity of women. However, Lamas's definition of this word brushes up against preexisting definitions in the United States. Historically, African American feminists have promulgated the term "womanism" and organized as "womanists," and some U.S. Latina feminists have organized under the umbrella term of "*mujerismo*" or as "*mujeristas.*" These terms have been used to signify particular kinds of U.S. women of color feminisms that stand in opposition to "mainstream," primarily white and middle-class feminist movements. Clearly, Lamas is using these terms in very different ways with disparate meanings than those commonly used in U.S. feminist circles. Thus, as the translator, the option that seems the most advisable is to leave the term "*mujerismo*" in the text while warning the reader ahead of time to distinguish between Lamas's ascribed meaning of the word and the word as used in the United States. As Lamas's work is translated into a U.S. context, it is important to realize the ways that some words in Spanish have attained independent and, in this case, contradictory meanings to those ascribed in Latin America.

Another instance where a note would seem to be pertinent is Lamas's use of the term *sexuación*. The translation of *sexuación* from the Spanish presents certain difficulties and has important theoretical implications. In an email conversation, Lamas explained the way she uses this term. For her, *sexuación* refers to the sexed, biological condition of males and females of the species. Gender would be the result of the social process by which females become women and males, men. Sexing is a verb (as in sexing the body), but, for Lamas, it gives the impression that there is a human action behind it. Gendering the body would attribute certain characteristics to particular bodies; however, sexuation (*sexuación*) is something that does not depend on human will, belonging in a Lacanian sense to the order of the real, like death itself. For these reasons, I have decided to use the term "sexuation" in English in this essay. This word is used in Lacanian contexts in English, as a translation of the French term *la sexuation*; some translators of ex-Lacanian psychoanalyst and critic Luce Irigaray have translated *sexuation* as "sexuation" or "sexualization" and her discussion of *droits sexués* as "sexuate rights." In other parts of this essay, the term *"sexuado"* in English is sometimes translated as "sexuated" and at others as "sexed." This reflects a suggestion by Lamas to vary the two terms in English depending on the specific case at hand.

It is perhaps worth mentioning that in Romance languages (and historically in English), the word for gender (in the case of Spanish, *género*) not only means gender but also genre, as in literary genre or other grammatical and taxonomic distinctions of class or type. While historically the word "gender" also had these implications in English, these connotations are less immediately present for most English speakers. In Spanish, this dual meaning presents an issue as the word does not have the immediate association with sexual difference that it has attained in English. This case of gender versus *género* highlights the different connotations of a word, which, on first glance, would seem to be a simple translation, presenting few problems. This intimate relationship between English and Spanish not only facilitates translation but can also simultaneously and in a contradictory way make it more perilous.

As is apparent in the text, Lamas assiduously follows feminist thinking and scholarship in the English language, recontextualizing these concepts within a Mexican and broader Latin American context. Nevertheless, until now, there has not been much possibility for a dialogue; Lamas reads and reinterprets without Anglophone feminists reading her work and responding to her ideas. This translation then opens up the possibility for a dialogic conversation to occur; however, as Gayatri Spivak mentions in her introduction to the series, the hope is that Anglophone readers will move toward the original languages of the texts, hopefully leading to a more multilingual, global conversation.

JOHN PLUECKER

Preface

The four essays compiled in this book seek to communicate my experiences, certain information, several critical reflections, and a number of debates. Ever since I first became aware of feminism in 1971—and I joined what at the time was known as "the Women's Liberation Movement"—I attempted to write about what was happening to me personally and on a broader level. Over the course of the years, some of these texts have circulated widely, above all as photocopies. Perhaps the point of publishing these today, along with an additional more recent essay, is to enable an old debate to reach new audiences.

I have chosen four very different texts that establish the boundaries of my work within feminism: the political development of a sector of the movement; affirmative action in the workplace; conceptual advances in regards to gender, and disagreements among feminists. Although all of these are part of a much more complex whole, they represent the breadth of my work through various stages of my feminist journey.

The first, "From Protesting to Making Proposals: Scenes from a Feminist Process," has evolved through several different versions since the eighties. I have been rewriting this article for the last twenty years, influenced by changing historical conditions, although its goal has remained the same: to record the trajectory of a single sector of feminism in Mexico City. Although I recognize from the outset my own bias in this story—since I am one of the protagonists—I think we need to shed light on what has occurred. The recording of life experience is a crucial aspect for transmission. Unfortunately, very few narratives like this have been written. My biased and surely partial perspective seeks to contribute to filling this informational vacuum not only with the story of my own participation, but also with the responses that—ideally—my reflections will provoke.

The second essay, "Equality of Opportunity and Affirmative Action in the Workplace," is a completely different piece than the first. It is an explanation of the logic behind affirmative action, with a short compilation of a few successful attempts to enact it in other countries. Antidiscriminatory policies in the workplace have been a central part of feminist political action. Knowing what has happened in other countries is fundamental if we are to make the most of other peoples' experiences and define our own demands better. This text has had wide circulation in official circles, and its transmission ended up being very effective. Above all, the essay is an example of feminism's insistence on strengthening the position of women in the public sphere; in addition, it identifies the challenges and pitfalls still faced by women in Mexico.

The third article, "Gender: Some Theoretical and Conceptual Advances," is an update on the debate surrounding this difficult and often misunderstood concept. The essay is a version of a keynote speech I delivered at the Symposium on Gender Studies at the Universidad Nacional Autónoma de México (UNAM) in 2004. In this speech, I attempted to explain the state of the gender question, while providing interpretive tools and clarifications on the use of the much-bandied-about concept of gender. It is the most recent essay and it condenses several of my theoretical concerns.

The fourth essay, "Feminisms: Disagreements and Arguments," was developed for a seminar with Latin American feminists. My main concern at the time was the apparent inability of feminists within the movement to listen to the reasoning of other feminists; it seeks to generate a dialogue, not only about internal issues, but also on issues in other areas. As the text initially was not intended for publication, but rather as a means of sparking internal debate, I was quite surprised to discover that the text was being used in several Latin American countries as a starting point for political discussions. Thus, I decided to distribute it more widely.

These essays are part of a practice of transmission and retransmission of feminism in which I have been involved in for many years. As is readily apparent, a book reveals one's intellectual trajectories. It would not be difficult to identify my own (psychoanalysis, Marxism, anthropology), since I have clearly been affected by the set of influences that comprise the sector of Mexican feminism that we could categorize as "leftist." Much of my discussion will concern our internal debates. The fact that many of my friends and adversaries have not committed their opinions to writing must have something to do with the sense of political urgency from which they have been unable to extricate themselves. Despite this, we cannot rule out the idea that some others, affected by pragmatism or frustrated by the difficult language of theory, have very little interest in the process of transmission.

The goal of this book is, therefore, two-fold: to reach those who are thinking and debating about the kind of society we wish to build, and second, to reach those who are taking action on a daily basis to build this other kind of society. It is worth mentioning that the transmission of knowledge, political experience, and discussions is a necessary step for new political agendas and debates to arise. This is the overriding objective of the book you have in your hands: to provide the building blocks for a more expansive agenda.

As part of this effort, I take for granted what George Steiner affirms in *Éloge de la transmission* (2003): that he is a professor and not a creator. I recognize myself in this distinction, although Steiner is light-years ahead of me. This is why I do not talk about creation: everything here was passed on to me by someone else, transmitted to me. And since I am convinced that an attempt at transmission founded on a critical, academic framework would, from the start, exclude many people, I have decided to keep the number of bibliographic references to a minimum, leaving those that are indispensable at the end of the book.

I would like to conclude this preface by acknowledging my debt to so many people. To those who make my daily life easier and thereby allow me to work: Diego Lamas, Francisca Miguel, Patricia Ramos-Saavedra, Ofelia Sánchez-Felipe, and Vicenta Sánchez-Felipe. To those who are at my side during feminist battles: my *compañeras* from *Debate Feminista*, from *GIRE*, from the Simone de Beauvoir Leadership Institute, from *Semillas*. To those who read me, correct me, and criticize me: Marta Acevedo, Lucero Gónzalez, Ana Luisa Liguori, Chaneca Maldonado, Patricia Mercado, Hortensia Moreno, María Teresa Priego, Raquel Serur, and last but not least, Carlos Monsiváis. I thank all of them, because if I am to remain active in theory and in practice, I need the support these individuals so generously provide me.

MARTA LAMAS

INTRODUCTION

Thinking Feminism from Mexico

Jean Franco

The Spanish title of Marta Lamas's book, *Feminismo: Transmisiones y Retransmisiones* (*Feminism: Transmissions and Retransmissions*), refers to an essay by George Steiner in which he describes himself as a transmitter rather than a scholar or a creator. All too often, in the past, transmission has been a one-way process radiating from the so-called center to the so-called periphery. Marta Lamas's essays represent a reverse process in that they critically evaluate forty years of feminist thinking in Europe and the Americas through the lens of activism and public debate in Mexico.

Nothing illustrates this breadth of vision better than the journal *Debate Feminista* (*Feminist Debate*), which she helped found in 1979 with an editorial board that included talented women scholars, writers, and performers. In naming the journal *Feminist Debate*, the editors promised an unbiased forum for discussion and "open questions," and the diversity of contributions and points of view reflected a decision to steer clear of sectarianism. Founded at a moment when, in Latin America, governments, including military governments such as that of Pinochet, were promoting the free market as the mechanism for growth, and ignoring the often brutal economic divisions, in particular the exploitation of women workers in sweat shops and assembly plants, *Debate Feminista* set out to define democracy as a central question for women. Democracy was and is a particularly important issue in Mexico. In many Latin American countries, especially those of the Southern Cone, "the return to democracy," even though in a limited form, was a welcome turn of events, coming as it did in the wake of the brutal and traumatic "cleansing" of military governments. But Mexico is a different and complex case. The country had been governed since 1929 by the Partido Revolucionario Institucional (The Institutional Revolutionary Party), a party that held on to power through a machine that effectively marginalized alternatives and was oiled by bribes and corruption. Presidents elected every six years chose their own successor from the inner cabal. This was effectively a one-party system, one that was shaken—though it was not overturned—by the student protests of 1968 on the eve of the Olympic Games held in Mexico City, a protest that included many women students marching on behalf of radical reform. When the army shot down and killed several hundreds of the demonstrators in Tlatelolco, demands for democratization were momentarily silenced.

At this time, a macho culture still kept most middle-class women in the home with little to do except supervise the exploited domestics while men were free to roam. Many middle- and upper-class men boasted of "la casa chica" (the second household) where they kept their lover and her children and that materially and symbolically was a confirmation of their sexual and financial success. The church, whose power had been greatly curtailed during and after the Revolution of 1910–17, not only regained influence but regulated women's social life from the pulpit and the confessional, from which conservative priests virulently opposed sexual diversity, abortion, and even (in the 1960s) miniskirts. A deep-rooted misogyny accounts for the unpunished violence against women, which is still endemic and which became a national and international scandal when, in the 1990s and in the first decade of this century, several hundred working-class women were raped, tortured, and killed in Ciudad Juárez near the frontier with the United States. With a police force indifferent to the rights of rape victims and victims of marital abuse, especially those of the lower class, and with a system that still favors impunity for male offenders, Mexico is a difficult battleground for feminists like Lamas and her colleagues who have taken on the fight not only for women's rights but also for the transformation of political culture and democratic practice.

The first women' s movements in Mexico were mobilized around the demand for voting rights, an uphill battle that finally succeeded in 1954. In the interim before the second wave of feminism, Rosario Castellanos, a writer, focused attention in poems and newspaper articles on the silence or indifference of middle-class women to their own humiliating situations. Castellanos's satirical plays, short stories, and numerous newspaper articles underscored the fact that middle-class women tacitly collaborated in their own oppression when they chose comfort over liberation, a comfort that they owed to domestic service. The servant was the mattress on which middle-class women comfortably reclined, Castellanos argued. Only "with the disappearance of the last servant will the first angry rebel appear." A decade later, many supporters of the second wave of feminism still comfortably reclined on the mattress as Marta Lamas points out in her essay "From Protest to Policy."

Transposed to Mexico, the US feminist slogan "the personal is the political" encouraged the separation of women's issues from the political. Writing of the wave of Mexican feminism that dates from the early 1970s and was strongly influenced by US and European feminism, Lamas argues that the "the personal is the political," taken over by several of the women's movements in the 1970s, was problematic in that as a slogan it allowed women to evade the broader political problems by opting out of the public sphere. This is why *Debate Feminista*, from the very beginning, proclaimed democracy to be an urgent issue in Mexico, a work in progress, and insisted that it was crucial for women to become involved in questions of class, ethnicity, health, employment, and religion as well as those specifically women's issues such as abortion, inequality, and male supremacy. Essays by Chantal Mouffe and Nancy Fraser, published by *Debate Feminista*, had argued that while feminists campaigned for a wide range of rights, they had done so without questioning the dominant liberal models of citizenship and politics. The very notion of citizenship and the public sphere as elaborated in European political thought assumed a universality that allowed it to pass over the exclusion of sectors of the population from citizenship in vast areas of the globe. In one of the essays published by *Debate Feminista*, Chantal Mouffe argued for radical democracy, pointing out that the distinction between private and public that had been central to the affirmation of individual liberty acted as a powerful principle of exclusion, while the liberal notion of the public sphere prevented the recognition of division and antagonism that had relegated particularity and difference to the private sphere. As an editorial in *Debate Feminista* put it, democracy must include a plurality of demands and could not exclude issues pertaining to blacks, to the indigenous and to homosexuals, and to the demands of social movements. In an effort to maintain their purity, some Mexican feminist organizations had refused to participate in the first United Nations International Women's Conference in 1975 on the grounds that the U.N. was imperialist. Yet the U.N. meeting had extraordinary repercussions in Latin America, principally because it exposed both the class and racial biases within feminism, and the absurdity of the classless discourse of US and European feminists. During the conference, there were vigorous protests by working-class and indigenous women, notably by the Bolivian miner's wife, Domitila Chungara, who vociferously objected to the middle-class leadership and exclusivity. This class and racial division would plague many future "encuentros" (meetings) of Latin American feminists. In Mexico, two events focused attention on the invisible underclass: the earthquake of 1985 and the uprising of the Zapatistas in Chiapas in 1994, two years after the quincentennial celebrations of Columbus's landing in the Americas.

By 1985, when the massive earthquake struck, Mexico City had become an unmanageable megacity, one of the largest in the world, its population swollen by immigration from the countryside. It housed illegal sweat shops in dilapidated areas in which a mostly female workforce was brutally exploited. It was these areas that the earthquake hit particularly hard. Elena Poniatowska, in her book of interviews with survivors, *Nothing Nobody: The Voices of the Mexico City Earthquake*, interviewed and recorded the stories of survivors that revealed the ruthless exploitation that the disaster had brought to light. Eight hundred garment workers were killed and about 40,000 left without work. As rescuers searched the rubble of some 800 sweat shops and factories, many of them clandestine and housed in shoddy buildings, what was striking was the capacity of neighborhood groups that included many women to organize the rescue operation, thus exposing the inadequate and tardy government response. The Nineteenth of September Garment Workers' Union, founded by mostly women workers, in an industry that had done its best to keep out unions, was one outcome of the earthquake.

A second major event with repercussions for feminists occurred in 2001, when the Tzozil woman and Zapatista commander Esther, wearing the black ski-mask of insurgency, addressed the Mexican Congress on behalf of indigenous women. Although of mainly symbolic significance, her appearance attracted national attention. She surprised the delegates by speaking to them as an indigenous woman who had experienced both racial and sexual discrimination at first hand. She drew attention to the fact that indigenous women, who formed a substantial contingent of the Zapatista army, had issued their own bill of women's rights, detailing discriminatory practices, including those within indigenous communities, where they were often excluded from decision-making and could not even decide how many children they could have. Both the Garment Workers' Union, formed after the earthquake, and the Zapatista bill of rights instructed Mexicans that feminism was not a middle-class luxury, and that poor and indigenous women could speak for themselves and engage in dialogue in the public sphere. Nongovernmental organizations (NGOs) would play an important role in the mobilization of working-class women and it is of some significance that at the Beijing Conference of 1995, some 250 Mexican NGOs participated in the parallel congress held in Hairou.

Calculated in terms of political participation in the face of great difficulties, the gains for women seem spectacular. Mexico has one of the largest contingents of women deputies in Latin America. Representation is now ensured through party quotas so that there is a substantial representation of women in the legislature. But even as I write this, on September 4, 2009, the newspaper *La Jornada* reports that eight women just elected have asked permission to hand over their seat to men. Thus the obstacles are still daunting. This was made very clear in 2000, when Vicente Fox, a candidate from the conservative National Alliance Party, was elected president. The election was widely celebrated as the end of one-party rule in Mexico and the president and his wife gave verbal support to some feminist issues, although party members and local officials attempted to clamp down on abortion rights and on the rights of gays and lesbians. More importantly, the government failed to intervene in one of the most scandalous atrocities involving women. Beginning in 1993, several hundred women, many of them assembly plant workers, had been cruelly tortured and killed in the northern city of Ciudad Juárez. The impunity of the assassins is widely attributed to a collusion between drug traffickers, prominent citizens, and corrupt police and local officials. As many of these women workers in the assembly plants were mestizas, often immigrating from other parts of the country, they reminded the public of the vulnerability of poor women workers and drew attention to the fact that "impunity" had reached scandalous proportions. In 2008, the United Nations Human Rights representative in Mexico, Amerigo Incalcaterra, resigned from his post citing the fact that unpunished attacks on journalists, indigenous peoples, and the unpunished assassination of women in Ciudad Juárez had made his work impossible. At the regional conference of Latin

American and Caribbean feminists in 2004, the Plataforma de Acción (Action Agenda) drew attention to the femicides in Mexico and other countries protesting both impunity and the model of development that exposed working women to abuse. In August 2009, the newspaper *La Jornada* published a report of the Human Rights Commission of Mexico State that gave the figure of 672 women assassinated in the course of the year. Eighty-nine percent of the cases were unsolved. The term "femicide" has been coined to deal with these hate crimes that, as the president of the Center for Human Rights stated, were particularly cruel in their chosen method. The women were not only raped but their bodies were also mutilated and abandoned.

Rape, especially of minors, poses another kind of problem when it results in pregnancy in a country where abortion rights have been fiercely opposed. The case of Paulina that gained national attention was particularly instructive in revealing the obstinate opposition in the face of nationwide protests. As a thirteen-year old, Paulina became pregnant after a thief broke into her home and raped her. When the doctors at a Mexicali hospital refused to perform an abortion, her cause was taken up by several women in the abortion rights movement and by prominent women, among them the writers Elena Poniatowski and Marta Lamas. Though they lost the battle, the coalition of supporters of abortion rights publicized their case. They would gain a significant victory when, in 2008, the Supreme Court of the State of Mexico would vote to legalize abortion in that state. While the victory is significant, nobody doubts the strength of the opposition. Following on the decrimininalization of abortion in the Federal District, the Right organized a campaign in fourteen states "to protect life from the moment of conception to natural death."

This paradoxical situation, in which women's organizations flourish while misogyny and violence against women and their exploitation seem as entrenched as ever, is the context in which Marta Lamas has operated since the 1970s. A realist, she knows that misogyny, deeply rooted in everyday practices and structures, will not end overnight.

Lamas is forthright in her criticism of identity politics and of forms of empowerment that rely on the discourse of victimization. She strongly supports women's political participation and the formation of pressure groups around specific demands. She opposes the idea that women's political participation means sacrificing their specific issues or capitulating to patriarchy. She encourages leadership training and promoting women candidates for office. Most recently, she has supported a new political party, which is in favor of, among other issues, diversity and abortion rights. What she would like to see is sexual and reproductive rights become fundamentally embodied "in democratic and republican practice." In a society dominated by machismo, feminists must, of necessity, be radical, must challenge existing structures of power, and must broaden the basis of citizenship. It is feminism, in such a context, that must also lead the way to less egoistic and self-centered identities that are more altruistic and in solidarity with one another. This may sound unduly optimistic but it is a conclusion arrived at through forty years of militancy.

The four essays included in *Debate Feminista* cover various aspects of her work—exemplifying the differences within Mexican feminism as they have developed historically, considering the US debates on equal opportunity and reverse discrimination and their possible application to Mexico, an examination of "gender" both in its everyday usages and in theory, and, in the fourth essay, the differences within feminism. In all the essays, the history and priorities of Mexican feminism are grounded in a carefully structured theoretical framework that she sets out in the third essay, in which she unravels the many usages of the term "gender" as well as its various deployments in discussions of theory. She argues that theory is not only essential to our understanding of the complexity of the symbolization of sexual difference but also for devising a workable political program. The word "gender," loosely used by international organizations and governments, has become an "epistemological cushion." Its use, both in everyday language and in theory, needs to be carefully examined. Theory, in her view, is handmaiden to political practice and necessarily encompasses both corporeality and its symbolization: psychic and social. As a trained anthropologist, she is clearly indebted to that discipline and to psychoanalysis for its contribution to an understanding of the symbolization of sexual difference that underpins the formation of subjectivities. Where she differs from many other theorists is in her insistence that understanding theory is vital for appropriate political action.

This said, her program for change may seem frankly utopian in the Mexican context. In the second essay, she presents the reader with an overview of the debates around equal opportunity and their practical results in the United States. When it comes to Mexico, however, equal opportunity is as a meaningless slogan unless it is accompanied by fundamental changes in the culture of the workplace and in social security, changes that would require the extensive mobilization of women, not to mention a fundamental reeducation of an entire political class.

In the final essay, she considers the internal debates in Latin American feminism that have led to acrimonious confrontations and personal quarrels that are symptoms of antiintellectual tendencies. She is forced to admit that feminist thinking has very little weight in the Latin American intellectual environment and that there is no recognition that theory might be a crucial guide to political action. Hence the conclusion: given that women are crucial to the project of redefining and promoting democracy, as long as they remain divided and unable to form coalitions or compromise, this crucial goal will remain unattainable.

There is a lesson here for other parts of the world. For despite all the talk of democracy, all assurances that Europe and the United States are democratic, it has yet to be fully realized in those bastions of enlightenment as well. Lamas remains required reading.

CHAPTER 1

From Protests to Proposals: Scenes from a Feminist Process

This chapter deals with a number of aspects of the Mexican feminist movement's process of political intervention. I analyze the way a certain political dynamic evolved and point out some changes that emerged following a strategic reorientation. Concretely, I explain how a sector of Mexican feminism moved from seeing politics as a masculine affair to reclaiming political work as something necessary and pertinent. This move from protesting to making proposals is evident in the increasing professionalization of feminist interventions in public life at a national level.

Basically, I look into two distinct moments in feminism in Mexico: the first, characterized by a conception that, idealizing the feminine condition romanticizes relationships between and among women and develops a politics rooted in identity. This conception is nourished by a way of thinking that aims to speak in the name of all women, what I call *mujerismo* (womanism).[1] The second moment is the gradual institutionalization of a number of organizational forms, with the goal of creating more effective and more pragmatic interventions in the public sphere.

In light of the fact that feminism reemerged publicly in Mexico in 1970, this essay covers thirty-five years, a historical period full of relevant processes.[2] For reasons of space, it would be impossible to cover everything that happened during this period; therefore, I will concentrate on the "political" aspect in this essay, and less so on the very important cultural dimension. Obviously, Mexican feminism is not one-dimensional, and the diversity of organizations, currents, and orientations within it prevents us from thinking of it as one sole process. Basically, I deal with the transformation of one sector of the movement, and even so, my version is just one among a number of other interpretations.[3]

This chapter arises out of my experience and is shaped by it. Because I have been an activist within the movement that I will analyze, I recognize at the outset that I am at risk of being biased in my reflections (Freud has already pointed out that memory is selective). Nevertheless, I am convinced that self-criticism is valuable in view of the enormous difficulties (both past and present) that feminists have faced in their attempts to develop concerted public efforts and an internal dialogue. Above all, I am interested in writing this story because the complexities of feminist participation have not been fully expressed in the few texts published on the subject. It would appear that Mexican feminists have serious problems recording their history, development, and debates. Just as "the vehemence of militancy leads to an inability to recognize what has been achieved,"[4] it also leaves little time to record life experience and little space for its conceptualization: there is nearly no written debate; no one draws up reports or provides their testimonies. This lack of publications prevents a critical analysis of the positives and the negatives of the movement's work, and as well impedes the development of rigorous and sustained political debate. The dearth of real intellectual debate also leads to an absence of collective reflection and internal criticism as it relates to feminists' enormous difficulties and their substantial successes in the development of coordinated public action.

The Refusal of Traditional Politics

In general, the idea that everything is political has prevailed within Mexican feminism. Since everything is connected to the exercise of power, politics is sometimes conceptualized as negotiation and administration. Both conceptions coexist simultaneously, intersect, and come into conflict. Thus, the distinction between the political and politics that Chantal Mouffe[5] has cited, based on the work of Carl Schmitt, is extremely relevant. She distinguishes between *the political,* which she considers the dimension of antagonism and hostility between human beings—antagonism expressed in multiple forms and arising from any type of social relationship—and *politics,* as the practice that seeks to establish an order and to organize human coexistence (in situations of great conflict, perpetually intersected by the political). Politics attempts to "domesticate" hostility and neutralize the political: the antagonism of power in human relationships.

The feminist tradition links politics with power in all contexts, in the sense that Mouffe identifies as political: wherever there is a relationship based on power, there is a political possibility that can be strengthened or interrupted. But, by associating politics with power, many activists develop a kind of denial of or disdain for any activity that results in agreement, administration, or political negotiation. By assuming this totalizing idea of the political—from which stems the classic feminist claim that the personal is political—a number of feminist groups turn away from the development of politics as a praxis and resist their own inclusion in the national political arena.

In addition, this takes place because feminists have constructed their political practice around their identity as women, giving precedence to an ideological and political discourse bordering on essentialism: "we are women;" "as women, we want," et cetera. This, while fostering group identification, makes a dialogue with national politics difficult, as has occurred with various groups in Mexico. However, I am getting ahead of myself. First, a review of the historical context is in order.

Gathering steam at the beginning of the 1970s, second-wave feminism was, at the start, embodied by middle-class women with university-level educational backgrounds who identified themselves with the positions of the Left and who were interested in the feminist debates going on in Europe and in the United States. These new feminists formed a social movement based on their critique of the sexual double standard and the role of the housewife, who was oppressed by the burdens of housework and raising children. In this manner, following the trail blazed by North American and European women, the incipient movement organized itself into consciousness-raising groups that were oriented toward the analysis and discovery of the female condition and that began with a discussion of their personal experiences, particularly in the area of sexuality. The slogan "The personal is political" completely reflected the spirit of the time. Because of these women's social backgrounds and since they had domestic workers to handle their housework and child rearing, the majority experienced feminism as a tool for analysis or for individual growth rather than as an organizational necessity for collectively confronting their own situation. Thus, Rosario Castellanos in 1971 stated that, "When the last maid disappears, when this buffer fostering our complacency is gone, then we'll see the first enraged, rebellious woman."[6]

The first activists established political relationships among themselves in a common space—the Coalition of Feminist Women (*Coalición de Mujeres Feministas*) (1976)—and voiced three main demands: voluntary maternity (which implied the right to sexual education, the use of contraceptives, and legal access to voluntary abortion), the end of sexual violence, and the right to free sexual choice. These demands became the principal axes around which their activism developed, and the movement increased its presence in the public sphere.

During the initial years, feminist groups were intensely involved in cultural criticism, which allowed them to display convincing evidence of sexism effectively. In this decade, several efforts were launched that, over the years, would multiply: in Mexico City, Alaíde Foppa started her program Women's Forum (*Foro de la Mujer*) on Radio UNAM, led the first academic seminar at the National Autonomous University of Mexico (UNAM) on the condition of women, and founded the magazine *Fem*, which remains in existence today. Along with *Cihuatl* and *La Revuelta*, feminist publications disseminated feminist ideas and principles. Also, the first support organizations were founded: the Support Center for Raped Women (*Centro de Apoyo a Mujeres Violadas*) and the Collective for Solidarity Action with Domestic Workers (*Colectivo de Acción Solidaria con Empleadas Domésticas*). In addition, feminist groups held all kinds of protests, conferences, and competitions, setting forth a variety of public demands. Feminist groups emerged in other states in Mexico. In 1979, the National Front for Women's Liberation and Rights (*Frente Nacional por la Liberación y los Derechos de las Mujeres,* FNALIDM) was founded, which was the first unified organization of feminist groups, unions, gay groups, and leftist political parties.

During its resurgence, the movement focused on challenging and denouncing the actions of the government and political parties, not on dialogue with those in positions of authority or on constructing political alliances. The feminist groups' organizational logic, in particular with regard to leadership and representation, was different from that employed by other political actors. Thus, they were not successful in translating their proposals into the language of political transactions or in making these comprehensible for other groups. One example: in 1975, the majority of feminist groups decided not to participate in the World Conference on Women or in activities sponsored by the Mexican government. They found the world conference to be an attempt at manipulation, and accused the United Nations of appropriating the feminist cause in order to reduce its power. While they refrained from participating, their absence was not noted, and the foreign delegations that inquired as to the existence of Mexican feminists were told "there are none." At the same time, Mexican feminists were meeting on the other side of the city in protest at an isolated "counter conference."[7]

As they rebuffed the traditional political structures, these initial groups withdrew into their own revolutionary utopia, and their discourse became tainted by an all-or-nothing logic. A notable part of this dynamic was a resistance to accept leaders. Even at that time, the prevalence of *mujerismo* made representativity a chronic problem, because it hindered the recognition of differences. If we are all the same, how do you distinguish one woman as a leader? The conflicts were exacerbated when a few individuals gained visibility in the public eye and were named movement leaders by the mass media. The visibility achieved by certain movement members, who were imposed as representatives by the communicative logic of the mass media, generated ill will and hostility among feminists. The refusal to delegate the movement's voice to a few women also concealed feelings of envy and rivalry and disheartened some women. Feminists failed to understand the benefits of having certain public figures embody the movement's goals. Without formal channels of communication, the movement's positions were not made known, or were manipulated by the mass media. With no visible leaders, feminist activity was rendered invisible.

Although, at different moments, feminist groups developed multiple initiatives and sought to build temporary alliances (for example, the coalition in 1976 and FNALIDM in 1979), because they did not establish political relationships with other forces, the movement was cut off from national politics. Furthermore, by organizing into identity-based groups, personal emotions such as erotic passion or romantic resentments advanced to the forefront. The movement was forced to deal not only with the political immaturity of its activists, but also with their relationship conflicts. Being politically marginalized, feminist groups were affected by a hidden web of intimate connections and personal slights, which intensified apparently irrational reactions. All of this meant that the movement's capacity to respond when faced with difficult situations was severely damaged, and the movement acquired a political presence in public space only on a few occasions.

The cost of focusing efforts on carving out space and finding recognition within the Left was very high. Many women, especially those who were in the Mexican Communist Party

(*Partido Comunista Mexicano*, PCM) and the Revolutionary Workers' Party (*Partido Revolucionario de los Trabajadores*, PRT), struggled with the macho closed-mindedness of their comrades. There were also disagreements and misunderstandings, as, for example when the Mexican Communist Party accused feminism of being a puppet of Yankee imperialism in its fight for abortion. Years later, in 1980, this same party would present a feminist legislative proposal in the Mexican House of Representatives (*Cámara de Diputados*) to legalize the termination of a pregnancy. Demands such as these for abortion or lesbian rights confronted Catholic prejudices that were deeply rooted in Mexican society; as a result, defending these causes hindered acceptance of the movement.

In addition, the absence of an internal democratic culture weakened the groups, because there was no way to handle the problems caused by the multiplicity of ideas and levels of consciousness. Moreover, feminists were not able to agree on the meaning of autonomy, a key word in the movement's lexicon, and because of this, many women removed themselves from more broadly based political processes, limiting their perspective. Within this context, certain pitfalls stemming from the structure of feminist demands obstructed consensus and unified action plans, thereby, the movement's political development. The difficulty of establishing nonpersonalized political relationships also ended up being practically insurmountable.

It is well known that psychological incentives and needs greatly affect the dynamics of collective action.[8] From the radicalized perspective of 1970s' feminism, "fighting" was an end in itself, and the outcome of the struggle was much less important. In this respect, many feminist activists were intoxicated with their own radicalness and dedication, happy to sacrifice time for their activism, intoxicated by "identity" and without a real interest in influencing the nation's public life. The *mujerista* (womanist) ideology, the viscerality of the experience, and the dynamics of being set apart from the rest of the world (within a small group of initiates) was, despite its complete ineffectiveness, very gratifying at a personal level. This was the reason for the disturbing persistence in many feminists of the two symptoms of identity-based self-absorption: victimism and narcissism. Because of the way in which women related to the world—love as the root of meaning, living for others—it was common for feminists to develop an amorous logic—"We all love each other, we are all equal"— which did not allow them to accept differences. This *mujerismo* was a crucial reason for resistance to accept leaders, which thereby made representativity a chronic problem.

With the intensification of these conflicts, the first stage of the feminist resurgence, which witnessed the rise of a number of different groups and projects to fruition, ended at the beginning of the 1980s. What came afterward was a period of internal restructuring and retraction. A substantial sector of the feminist movement distanced themselves from internal fragmentation, passionate identification with sectarian viewpoints, and a reluctance to collaborate with people espousing different opinions. Rather, they turned to a model of interest groups that emphasized equality of rights in the legal sphere and that worked politically as advocates and lobby groups.[9]

Instead of small consciousness-raising groups, the array of feminist activity was centered on new models of committed activism, especially with salaried positions in groups structured as nonprofit organizations. After facing the constraints of financial survival, they formed nongovernmental organizations (NGOs) and applied for financial assistance from international agencies. But the funds that they received were not meant for developing a feminist infrastructure,[10] but, instead, for projects to combat poverty, which implied direct assistance to working-class and female agricultural workers. This gave rise to a tendency called "popular feminism," made up primarily of socialist feminists, Christian women, and former leftist party activists, which favored expanding the base of the grassroots women's movement.[11]

Feminists of multiple political orientations formed issue-based support networks, such as, for example, the Network Against Violence Toward Women (*Red Contra la Violencia a las Mujeres*), the Feminist Agricultural Worker Network (*Red Feminista Campesina*), and the Network of Popular Educators (*Red de Educadoras Populares*). Structures of institutionalized movements, such as the Coalition and the FNALIDM, ceased to serve as spaces for discussion and definition of common strategies. An important function of these coordinating networks was to spark the creation of an awareness of the need for national networking across the breadth and width of the country. Despite the weakened state of Mexico City–based feminists, the networks gave rise to *encuentros* (meetings)[12] in other regions of the country and a series of very meaningful dialogues and alliances with academic institutions, union locals, and a number of government workers, all of whom were sensitive to the demands of the popular women's movement. The feminists who focused their work on the popular sectors took advantage of the national and sectorial conferences of women workers, *campesinas* (female agricultural workers), and *colonas* (women involved in the national squatters and land rights movement), as well as local or regional meetings of popular women's groups, not only to exchange experiences, but also to debate the class and gender characteristics of the women's demands. Through this work, "popular feminism" took up the feminist demands of the 1970s once again and connected them with the specific demands of working-class women.

As "popular feminism" grew, it did not seek to impose a particular direction for popular actions, but to introduce feminist critical thinking. In a parallel manner, this feminist thought was beginning to be institutionalized in academic settings, such as the Interdisciplinary Program in Women's Studies (*Programa Interdisciplinario de Estudios de la Mujer*, PIEM) in 1982 at the Colegio de México, the Area for Women and Culture (*Área de Mujer y Cultura*) in 1983 at the Universidad Autónoma Metropolitana-Xochimilco (*UAM-Xochimilco*), and later, the University Program in Gender Studies (*Programa Universitario de Estudios de Género*, PUEG) at the UNAM in 1991.

The Crisis Facing Feminist Politics

In 1985, the earthquake that shook Mexico City gave rise to the spontaneous self-organization of the citizenry with significant leadership from women in working-class neighborhoods (housewives and salaried female workers). The popular movement of women in marginal areas of the city came into contact with feminists, since some of the latter reached out to the former to work in conjunction with them in their organizing and to introduce the feminist perspective into their organizations.[13] These popular organizations became an alternative form of participation for thousands of women; nevertheless, the demands around which they mobilized did not include the three basic demands of feminist demands: legalized abortion, a rejection of sexual violence, and respect for sexual diversity, this despite the fact that this sector of the population was precisely that which suffered most from the consequences of lack of sexual education, penalization of abortion, and the abuses of sexist violence.

Without going into an in-depth analysis of the composition and the reach of these feminist interventions, a relevant outcome of their political impact between 1985 and 1986 is noteworthy: many feminists recognized the need for specific negotiations on civic and/or union issues, and this slowly changed the feminist conception of politics, especially regarding their relationship with the state. A clear example was their work with seamstresses.[14] The Feminist Solidarity Committee (*Comité Feminista de Solidaridad*) made supporting them its main goal, first in the "September 19th" Cooperative, and later in the "September 19th" Union. However, the inability to reconcile the diversity of feminist positions provoked a crisis; conflicts over internal democracy, leadership, and pluralism weighed heavily on attempts to strengthen the work with these groups over the long term.

In this way, in addition to the long-standing problem of leadership or representation, feminist groups faced the challenge of working in conjunction with other political actors. In order to stimulate a more adroit conception of politics and to develop more effective forms of organization, a fundamental political understanding was necessary: the need for dialogue. Women for whom their own identity was sacred were not able to negotiate: these women saw themselves as total victims, or believed that deep down, they were more honest, more sensitive, and better than men. These victims and heroines were unable to build political relationships with each other or with other people.

This difficulty was apparent at the Fourth Feminist Conference of Latin America and the Caribbean (*IV Encuentro Feminista Latinoamericano y del Caribe*) that was held in Taxco in 1987, a space where the different political paradigms of feminism confronted each other. A central conflict during preparations for the conference was defining the nature of the meeting: Could all women attend, or were they required to be feminists? While the "popular" feminists defended the participation of all women, women from other sectors of the movement voiced the need for their own space in which to debate the feminist political agenda. Finally, it was agreed to respect plurality and to accept the participation of all women who considered themselves feminists. Although the coordinating group was able to prevent one tendency from dominating, the clash among the different sectors of the movement persisted.

More than 1500 women went to Taxco and discussed all kinds of topics: from identity, and the body, to alliances and proposals to build political strength. In reality, there were two parallel conferences. The majority of participants came from an influx of women in political organizations, militants in popular movements, mothers of the disappeared, cadres of *campesina* and union organizations, Christian women influenced by liberation theology, groups of women in exile, visual artists, New-Age women, and a huge number of Central American women involved both in the wars and in the politics of their respective countries. The strength of popular feminism was obvious; at the same time, there was little participation by middle-class women, although paradoxically the active minority—the "leaders"—of the feminist movement came from this class.[15]

A proposal to unify the two tendencies was made in a critical document developed by a handful of "historical" feminists.[16] This document sought (1) to provoke the recognition of difference and conflict in the political practice of the movement, (2) to recognize the exercise of power within the latter, and (3) to accept it as a source of transformation.

The document proposed the existence of ten intersecting and self-perpetuating myths[17] that shaped a way of thinking that in turn lead to weak and ineffectual political practice. These myths were evidence of the general tone of feminist politics in the region; they dominated the collective imaginary of the movement and contained the precepts of an identity-based politics that rendered an effective political strategy impossible due to its militant egalitarianism. The myths were also expressions of *mujerismo*, which on myriad occasions turned small feminist groups into suffocating ghettos in which complacency prevented criticism and growth; in these spaces, it was impossible to recognize differences in order to establish some representatives. For this reason, the document presented an implicit threat for a number of women who lived their feminism as a space of very deeply entrenched identity-based belonging.

Why does identity have such a mobilizing power? Why does it produce a cult of victimization? Pietro Barcellona argues that, in fact, the "terrain for the recovery of subjectivity is the existence of suffering." The mechanism driving this victimization consists of gaining self-consciousness through pain: "I am a certain person because I have experienced pain."[18] The identity politics of many social movements begin with equating oppression with authentic knowledge, and even with virtue: I live this discrimination, I know what it is like, and I am virtuous because I suffer. Barcellona points out: "Suffering cannot become the content of a proposal." It is impossible to rid the world of suffering, in that as human beings, we will always be exposed to it as a fundamental experience (our needs, losses, and sorrows). Pretending that suffering is a foundation for political proposals leads to anti-intellectual and populist positions that hinder the development of a shared civic consciousness.

Another characteristic of identity politics is that it leads to a "divided consciousness,"[19] which on the one hand, incorporates a feeling of harm and victimization and, on the other, a feeling of identity that leads to *empowerment*[20] and personal growth. This facilitates feminist identity-based demands, but obstructs the development of a broader based political practice, which is needed to gain additional ground, to achieve civic demands, or to build unifying forms of organization.

This in no way means that questions of identity should be silenced or denied; however, the sense of social connection must be founded on different terms. One must be conscious of the essentialist risk of speaking solely in identitarian terms, as in, for example: "we women." It is fully legitimate to claim identity, but only after taking into consideration the multiplicity of discourses and the power relations that intersect it. Moreover, there are no monolithic identities; they are, rather, all multiple and fractured. Singular identities are always mythical constructions. "Woman" does not exist; other identities intersect it: a young, indigenous, evangelical, *campesina* woman is not the same as an older, white, urban, atheistic, university woman. When we distinguish between different identity constructions, it is possible to see that, at certain times, some identities are more meaningful than others. This allows us to question the idea of a sole identity, one that supposedly has only one singular meaning.

The identitarian conception of feminism caused a crisis in Taxco in 1987, and for that reason, many feminists experienced the criticism as a personal attack and a sort of treason or deviation from a supposed feminist "essence." At this conference, when a perception arose that "the other women" were those who denied their essentialist feminist identity, the relationship between "us" and "them" turned into a friend–enemy relationship, that is, an antagonistic relationship.

In the realm of collective identifications, the differences between the two largest tendencies ("radicals" and "popular feminists") deepened, and opposition was formed between "utopic feminists" and "feminists of the possible."[21] This division would later be referred to as the opposition between "autonomous feminists" and "institutional feminists."[22] When we reconceptualize political practice, characterizing identity not as an irreducible essence but rather as a position that we assume or that is assigned to us, we replace the question "Who am I?", which is present in some defenses of diversity, with the question "Where am I?" Focusing on place allows us to see the people around us. The emphasis on the where—on the position—facilitates thinking in a different way about questions of identity.[23] For example, thinking about location encourages a concern with the relationships among diverse kinds of identities and, therefore, with the development of a politics based on affinities and coalitions.

The fight against exclusionary versions of identity-based claims requires another type of identification—which we may call civic—that is, one that is faithful to pluralism and democratic values. In this regard, Chantal Mouffe describes the constitution of identity stemming from a multiplicity of interactions; because it is always a process that weaves very complex relationships among a variety of identification types, identity ends up as an intricate network of differences, a process. Mouffe poses another dilemma: all difference is based simultaneously on opportunity for union and on political antagonism, since it is sufficiently strong to provoke an effective regrouping of people into two groups: people who are the same, and people who are different. This is the great dilemma of diversity. For this reason, the defense of the project of democracy demands we consider the very nature of human diversity. How are we to confront diversity, the multiplication of particularisms, and the emergence of new antagonisms? We can situate ourselves within the broader context of the paradoxes of pluralist democracy, and not deceive ourselves with the illusion of a consensus that would definitively eliminate diversity. According to Mouffe, the risk of pluralist democracy being undermined by a lack of civic identities leads to the multiplication of conflicts employing essentialist, identity-based terms, with its nonnegotiable moral values. This is the negative cost of identity-based neocorporativism.[24]

As the Taxco crisis took place within the context of the debate on the huge mobilization prior to the 1988 elections, several feminist groups became increasingly concerned about their participation. At the time, there was increasing understanding of the need to take part in the political life of the country. Previously, the movement did not have proposals for a democratic transition, nor had it taken into consideration the opening of spaces as a result of the political reform begun by the state. A broad sector of the movement held a view, originating in Marxism, of feminism as a "revolutionary" option; for this group, there was no reason to get involved in the fight for democracy, since it was a reformist cause. Therefore, the movement issued no public statements during the previous two presidential elections (1976 and 1982) and feminists did not establish alliances or support candidates, nor did they demand that candidates state their positions on feminist demands. Although the movement also refrained from taking such steps in 1988, at least there was a proposal to incorporate specifically feminist issues in the electoral agenda.

In addition, the need to participate in the country's political mainstream led several feminists to join the recently formed Party of Democratic Revolution (*Partido de la*

Revolución Democrática, PRD), which was made up of PCM and PRT members, and those of other leftist organizations. In the 1988 elections, when the early vote count favored PRD candidate Cuauhtémoc Cárdenas, the government's computer system unaccountably crashed and in the end, the final count designated the party in power the winner. After this electoral fraud, a significant number of feminists felt an urgent need to find ways to express their dissatisfaction.

The Political Rearticulation of the Movement

At the beginning of the 1990s, a series of events and national and international trends converged, and feminism attained a visible political profile for the first time. At a national level, the transition process to democracy ended the monopolistic rule of the PRI party that had governed every state of the country for more than seventy years, and led to a realignment of feminist activism in other spaces. After the 1988 electoral fraud, new areas are opened up in terms of civic consciousness, and many feminists felt the urgent need to find new channels to express their dissatisfaction.[25] They began to reevaluate their relationship with politics, to develop mechanisms for participating in the realpolitik, to establish alliances, to influence electoral outcomes, and to build a shared agenda. When the Left also reevaluated the role of representative democracy, a new openness emerged regarding the relationship with the state. This led to a significant shift in attitudes: a sector of the movement accepted the political agreement as a responsible tool of democracy. The 1990s quickly became the decade of agreements. This led to new organizational styles—joining governmental committees, working as independent consultants for politicians and parties, building alliances with female bureaucrats and politicians—and a republican aspiration slowly began to emerge.

Disappointed by the failure to establish a Feminist Coordinating Committee that would be able to, on the one hand, respond publicly in a more systematic way, and on the other, to serve as a liaison, many feminist activists became involved in the national political scene through civic participation. While in the 1970s and 1980s, the anti-PRI spirit of the majority of feminists translated into an antigovernment stance opposed to any joint action with governmental agencies, in the 1990s, ideas about civic participation provoked the need to influence public policy. This was expressed in three efforts, two of which were associated with the founding triad of demands that united the movement: violence and abortion. First, the experience of working on issues of sexual violence, the only "respectable" demand, approvingly taken up across the entire political spectrum (including the right), redefined the alliances with women in the government and the state apparatus, and enriched political agreements between women. In 1991, an advocacy group was created made up of feminists, congresswomen, female academics, and female bureaucrats in order to introduce reforms to the law on sexual crimes: the Plural Group (*el Grupo Plural*). The law passed thanks to the group's lobbying and to the alliance of congresswomen of all the parties, coordinated by Amalia García, then a PRD congresswoman.

The second effort raised the issue of quotas. At the beginning of the decade, a sector of "popular" feminism initiated a more pragmatic intervention in the public sphere and discovered that more women were needed in political positions. This group demanded quotas for female representation to correct the political parties' numerical imbalance. The PRD was the first to modify its statutes, establishing that there should not be more than 70% of males in the party's leadership.[26] "Gaining spaces" ("*Ganar espacios*") was the slogan of the campaign for affirmative actions; this was decided at the Seventh National Feminist Conference (*VII Encuentro Nacional Feminista*) held in Acapulco in 1992. After this conference, the aforementioned campaign was launched, aimed at building alliances with women in the government and in the state apparatus and prioritizing political agreements among women.

The third effort was related to decriminalization of abortion. After more than twenty years of demanding "free and legal abortion" with no success, a group of feminists modified their discourse, demanded reforms, and addressed their arguments both to the society as a whole and to decision-makers.[27] Viewing abortion as the pivotal point for women's freedom and autonomy and confronting the parties' resistance to this legal change, these feminists proposed new forms of civic participation in the issue. In 1993, the international climate bolstered this transformation through a variety of preparative activities for the Conference on Population and Development to be held in Cairo in 1994. Considering themselves to be part of a global movement, several members of feminist NGOs used this same strategy to influence the government by their decisive participation on the international political stage. Both UN conferences, that is, Population and Development (Cairo, 1994) and the Fourth World Conference on Women (Beijing, 1995) were very useful, because demands silenced at a national level—like that of abortion—became objects of discourse in international forums and forced governments to take positions.

The coalition of nongovernmental groups called "For a Feminist Millennium" that brought together 260 NGOs from throughout the country (more than half of the 500 on record working with women) stated that ratifying the Cairo platform in Beijing was a central task of the movement, because of the considerable advances in the area of reproductive health. "For a Feminist Millennium" held meetings in different Mexican states and opened a space for dialogue and intergroup negotiation. Several feminists formed part of official delegations at these UN conferences, thus gaining experience in lobbying and organization and in building awareness about international feminism's capabilities.

In addition, the debate stemming from these UN conferences legitimized feminist discourse on the national political stage as the "gender perspective."[28] *Gender* went mainstream in the 1990s; it became a way of understanding the sociocultural origin of women's subordination and the power imbalance that infuses relations between the sexes.[29]

In 1993, the group "From A to Z" (*De la A a la Z*) was founded, composed of seven feminists with distinct center-left stances: two from the PRD; two from the PRI, and three politically independent feminists.[30] To introduce themselves to the public, they decided to hold a commemoration of the fortieth anniversary of women's obtaining the vote, in which they made public their proposal for women to "Take a Step Forward" (*"avanzar un trecho"*) before political differences separated them.[31] "From A to Z" emphasized the need for alliances and agreements among women and, several years later, this discourse would yield notable successes.

As part of feminist activism's "outward" realignment, the impact of the emergence of the Zapatista Army for National Liberation (*Ejército Zapatista de Liberación Nacional*, EZLN) in January 1994 in Chiapas, one of the states with the largest indigenous populations and greatest poverty level, reenergized a sector of the movement. The EZLN made its feminist inclinations clear when it proclaimed the Women's Revolutionary Law (*Ley Revolucionaria de las Mujeres*), which recognized the right of women to full political participation—including taking on political and military leadership roles—in addition to their right to decide on all aspects of their lives—the choice of marriage, number of children, and paid work—as well as condemning physical and sexual violence against women. Several feminists approached the Zapatistas and built bridges of collaboration.

The ideas circulating about civic participation fostered a need to take action, and the pro-Zapatista wing was active, channeling the interests and the political development of many feminists. Between 1994 and 1996, different collective pluralist coalitions were formed: a national feminist-movement network (Feminist Millennium, *Milenio Feminista*), a forum for strategic debate (the Women's Convention, *la Convención de Mujeres*), a large space for the union of women of all stripes, from pro-Zapatistas to PAN members (the Assembly of Women, *la Asamblea de Mujeres*), and the first national feminist political association (Diverse, *Diversa*). In addition, many feminists joined mixed civil organizations with civic demands, such as the Civic Alliance (*Alianza Cívica*), and also fought for a space in the political parties. Nevertheless, an enormous gap persisted between abundant participation and almost nonexistent representation, and many feminists became aware of the paradox inherent in lack of recognition of their leadership.

At this point, this sector of the movement was well aware that politics as an exercise in ideological purity or autonomy at all costs does not foster democratic relationships. The other part of the movement still perceived participation in traditional politics as intensely problematic. These feminists have exchanged their old fear of government cooptation for the new fear of the mediatization of feminist groups seeking to institutionalize themselves. Faced with the opposition between radicalism and reformism, the old demand for autonomy became quite relevant again.[32] Some women approached autonomy from an eminently separatist perspective, exhibiting their fear of possible "assimilation" or "adulteration" of feminist propositions; other women defended a notion of autonomy that incorporates a diversity of participants in the political relationship, favors coalitions, and seeks to wield influence in a politically effective way without losing sight of its principles. Between these two stances there were many nuances. But leaving autonomy undefined or confusing political autonomy with organizational autonomy gave rise to a dynamic of intolerance. As a result, there was scant possibility for internal dialogue or for the formation of proposals for unified action.

This opposition between "revolutionaries" and "reformists" reflected the distinction made by Mouffe between the conceptions of the political and politics: some viewed feminism as a weapon to confront the political; for this reason, public intervention was seen as a threat that would neutralize the radical "essence" of feminist demands. Resentments and paranoia were intertwined with what appeared to them to be a contemptible option: political negotiation, experienced as meaning both treason and a "scam" of the "system." In addition, one must not forget that for many feminists, reformism tarnished the heroism of revolutionary activism.

For their part, feminists convinced of the need to participate in politics spoke out in favor of the idea of politics as a negotiation of conflicts. But, although they no longer idealized feminist politics as they redirected their radicalism into democratic practices, feminists were still not entirely free of conflicts or revolutionary nostalgia. Many continued to be trapped in absurd rivalries, since identitarian logic brought women of multiple political stripes into conflict, simply because they belonged to different networks or groups. These failings were a consequence of "identity politics," since it mixed political concerns with concerns of daily life without the necessary separation between doing and being. As a result, discursive dislocations, false oppositions, and personalized confrontations emerged.

In many groups, a paradoxical situation arose: the voice of the victim was not being heard, while at the same time, activists and supporters perpetuated an irritating, victimistic discourse. In particular, one serious failing was the lack of nonfeminist women debating about what sexism meant practically and politically. Despite filtration of the political and philosophical dimensions of feminism into daily life, the fight for decriminalization of abortion and recognition of sexual diversity had made the political acceptance of the movement more difficult. Concretely, although prominent intellectuals, scientists, and artists had supported the fight for legalization of abortion,[33] there were no groups of ordinary women mobilized around this crucial demand. Although there was an understanding that women had to take control over their own bodies in order to stop being victims, there was considerable resistance to positions stigmatized by the hegemonic ideology of the Catholic Church.

While confrontations persisted among some of the feminist groups, the so-called gender perspective acquired great resonance in political discourse. Its use in the public sphere, imposed by institutions such as the World Bank and the UN, contributed to the recognition of a specific set of problems and to the acceptance of the need to put leveling mechanisms into place. This was due in part to the leadership that women acquired in the last years of the twentieth century, as they occupied more public positions than ever before and achieved a growing political presence. Instead of a clear proposal for affirmative action, what emerged was embarrassment about the exclusively masculine composition of certain spaces of power. This is why the government created the National Program for Women (*Programa Nacional de la Mujer*) in 1996 as a part of an effort to reach the same level of gender equity as countries in the developed world.

For the first time, one sector of the feminist movement proposed candidates for positions in the program, and several feminists agreed to represent the feminist movement in its two agencies: the Council and the Comptroller's Office. Several days later, during the Feminist Congress for Social Change (*Congreso Feminista por el Cambio Social*) in 1996, these appointments were referred to as an achievement of the movement. Recognizing these posts as a collective victory rather than as individual cooptation (as this would have been interpreted previously) reflected a shift in the movement's political mentality.

At this point, a series of interesting changes took place. In 1997, *Diversa* called for all political parties to sign an agreement for equity entitled "Let's Take a Step Forward" (*"Avancemos un trecho"*). At a solemn event held at the Federal Electoral Institute, the six political parties in existence at the time (PRD, PRI, PAN, PPS, PT, and PVEM) signed the agreement. A little while later, the Federal Electoral Institute recommended a 30% quota for women in political parties; the House of Representatives (*Cámara de Diputados*) established the Commission on Equity and Gender (*Comisión de Equidad y Género*). In 1998, the "Women's Parliament" was founded—a legislative commission made up of senators and federal congresswomen whose goal was to open a space for reflection, deliberation, and promotion of a legislative agenda and of public policies that sought to end discrimination against women and to foster democracy. In 1998, the National Program for Women (*Programa Nacional de la Mujer*) was replaced with the National Commission on Women (*Comisión Nacional de la Mujer*) that, in 2000, became the National Institute of Women (*Instituto Nacional de las Mujeres, Inmujeres*), with more power, at least symbolically.

The Temptation of Politics

At the beginning of the twenty-first century, many feminists took a more pragmatic view of the intervention in politics and recognized that the progress of feminism is concerned not only with increased popular participation, but also with the need to assume positions in party, legislative and governmental structures. In 1999, the national organization *Diversa*, in existence since 1996, achieved the legal status of a national political group (*Agrupación política nacional*, APN), granted by the Federal Electoral Institute. An APN is one step below a political party and, in addition to other requirements, must have at least 7,000 people in its ranks. *Diversa* included feminist issues in its agenda, such as decriminalization of abortion, attention to sexual and reproductive health, and respect for sexual diversity.

At the same time, the emergence of new political contexts, with friends and allies in power, both improved the environment and made it more complex. The triumph of the leftist opposition (PRD) in Mexico City in 1997 changed the perspectives of many feminists who, tired of merely stating their values, now desired more activity. Several feminists moved into positions in PRD party and governmental structures. As part of this process, the enthusiasm sparked by the arrival in 1999 of Rosario Robles as interim head of government of the federal district (*Jefatura del Gobierno del Distrito Federal*) was particularly significant; Robles remained in this position of interim governor until 2000. A leftist university graduate and a UNAM union movement leader, Robles was characterized by a feminist discourse and carried out several feminist interventions during her period in office. Perhaps the one that caused the most publicity and scandal was a reform to Mexico City abortion laws, which introduced two exceptions to the criminalization of abortion: in cases of serious harm to the woman's health and of fetal abnormalities. (Mexico City's penal law on abortion dated from 1931. Some states had already reformed their law, enacting those two excluding clauses.) The reform was attacked as "unconstitutional" by the conservative National Action Party (*Partido de Acción Nacional*, PAN), but sixteen months later, the National Supreme Court of Justice (*Suprema Corte de Justicia de la Nación*) resolved the controversy by upholding the constitutionality of the so-called Ley Robles.

In 1999, the Simone de Beauvoir Leadership Institute (*Instituto de Liderazgo Simone de Beauvoir*, ILS) was founded as a space for training feminist leaders. Soon, in addition to leaders of feminist organizations and feminist government officials, women from other arenas arrived: city council members; mayors; indigenous leaders, and congresswomen. Designed as a space where intellectual work would be valued and focused primarily on other feminists, the institute gradually broadened its scope. In this same year, several feminists created the Consortium for Parliamentary Dialogue and Equity (*Consorcio para el Diálogo Parlamentario y la Equidad*), a civic organization with the goal of following the debates in Congress and the Senate in order to inform the feminist movement about the work of their political representatives and to introduce initiatives to reform laws. Several members of the consortium were active in *Diversa*, and in 2000 they proposed the establishment of a "Pact between Women: Towards a Legislative and Governmental Agenda for Equity" to all of the women candidates for Congress.[34] Women from civic, political, and social organizations all signed the agreement in an attempt to build a relationship of joint responsibility between the citizenry and legislative and governmental institutions.

For its part, *Diversa* achieved an unprecedented agreement with three parties. As a result, three candidates proposed by *Diversa*—a federal-level PRI congresswoman, a political representative in Mexico City (Iztacalco) from the PRD-PCD, and an assemblywoman in Mexico City for Social Democracy (*Democracia Social*)—won in the 2003 elections. At the same time, *Diversa* members participated in the construction of a new political party with a clear commitment to feminism.

In 2000, for the first time in seventy-eight years of one-party rule, a party other than the PRI won the federal elections. Despite recognizing the importance of alternation in office, many feminist groups bemoaned the victory of the National Action Party (PAN) because of its conservative politics. In his inaugural address, President Vicente Fox expressed his commitment to adopt the so-called gender perspective in his administration, summarily kissing a crucifix! Fox appointed three women as members of his cabinet;[35] only one of these remained in office: the minister of social development, Josefina Vázquez-Mota. A few feminists accepted positions in the new government, thinking they would take advantage of the new spaces supposedly opened by the alternation in office. While the majority of feminists awaited the

PAN's political line with skepticism, Fox's wife burst energetically onto the public scene. Marta Sahagún and what was to become her excessive prominence triggered a political debate regarding women, power, and, very concretely, the role of the so-called First Lady.[36] The appropriation of certain aspects of feminism by conservative female politicians is inevitable. This occurred in the case of Sahagún, who included various feminist issues in her discourse and attempted a rapprochement with several feminists. Mexico's First Lady confessed publicly to having been beaten by her previous husband and spoke about women's "empowerment" (*"empoderamiento"*), which provoked broad-based sympathy from women across the country. Her name soon rose to the top of the electoral polls.

The recently formed National Institute of Women (*Inmujeres*) ended up in the hands of a PAN member, who received Sahagún's support. Although one goal of several feminist groups was to exert an effect on the government's definition of public policies, they confronted the fact that Inmujeres was not the best space to accomplish this. Unable to define a public policy that dealt with women's basic problems, the institute was sadly ineffective due to its tepid conservatism. The institute did not even apply pressure to resolve the one demand to which the Right did not object—the fight against violence. Inmujeres did not push for a resolution to one of the most painful and scandalous national traumas: the murders of poor women, many of them teenagers, in the northern border city of Ciudad Juárez. After ten years of death and terror, the hate crimes, a type of "sexual hunting" continued, with no resolution.[37] The appointments of a special prosecutor and of a special commissioner with the task of monitoring the twenty points formulated to rebuild the "social fabric" of the city were only symbolic acts by the federal government. The new posts evidenced no real interest in getting to the root of the problem or in defeating the police and political corruption that impeded (and continues to impede) finding a resolution to the more than 300 femicides.

Cases such as those of Ciudad Juárez are a reminder of a terrible reality: broad sectors of Mexican women have not attained the living conditions of urban middle-class women. Because the distribution of wealth (material and symbolic) continues to be deeply unequal, the poorest women have hardly any chance to overcome their poverty, since they lack the resources to integrate themselves into the modernizing process that, paradoxically, creates wealth and exclusion at the same time.[38] In this regard, inequality among women is a gap that is not breached by the elimination of sexist discrimination, because, in addition to everyday machismo, there is the appalling distribution of resources and opportunities. Therefore, the movement must work to draw attention to the structural problems that persist and that prevent all women from achieving access to better life circumstances and to higher levels of participation. In addition, since the poorest women face absolutely precarious living conditions, the fight for daily subsistence overshadows interest in any other issue. Due to the fact that the economic dynamics set up conditions that are difficult to overcome, social pressure becomes the only way to compel political parties to incorporate a real gender perspective that includes specificity of social class and ethnic origin.

Although the horizon is not equally promising for all Mexican women, political, demographic, and workplace changes have modified women's social position and have laid the groundwork for the transformations that feminism has attained in other countries. The internationalization of new patterns of masculinity and femininity fosters more egalitarian lifestyles, types of work, and consumption models. More information produces better political practices and discourses. Thanks to the globalization of these new social, cultural, and political patterns, organized women's groups have more opportunities to take action, joining global networks to push their specific demands.

Faced with this state of affairs, the challenge for many feminists is to become a political force capable of offering concrete alternatives for participation. This means that the task ahead is twofold: both the need to reach out to the large numbers of women suffering from sexism in silence and isolation, and also the urgent necessity of advancing broad-reaching, nonsexist politics. This implies much more than modifying the distribution of workloads, schedules, and social tasks that take sexual difference and gender into account: it means showing, in each instance, in each situation, what happens to women and what happens to men. And, likewise, this presupposes accepting sexual difference at the heart of political organizations and in their daily tasks. Therefore, the great test to ascertain whether feminists are truly democratic political subjects is the inclusion of men in feminist thinking, discourse, and action.

In 2002, this way of thinking brought about the creation of a political party with a feminist orientation: México Posible. Patricia Mercado was the leader of the party, attracting environmentalists, gays, and human rights defenders. With support from different civic networks, the party ran candidates for Congress in 2003, but did not achieve the two percent of the vote necessary for legal standing. This same year, the Federal Electoral Institute made the quota of 30% of women mandatory in political parties, which it had recommended years before. The results were clear: from 16% of women in

2000, participation grew to 21% in 2003. The aim now is for women to take on leadership positions and not, as has occurred frequently, interim or substitute positions.

In 2003, Rosario Robles took up the proposal of the "From A to Z" group to establish connections among women of different political parties, and organized a plural celebration of the fiftieth anniversary of women's suffrage. This time, the political spectrum of the alliance was broadened to include members of the PAN. Twenty-one women of different political alignments and origins, who had known each other for years, came together at Robles's home. There were profound political disagreements among them, but nevertheless they were at the same place, willing to organize a celebration together. The relationship between these women was not one of love, but rather of necessity. News of the meeting leaked out to the press. The idea that "as women we still have to take this important step forward together, before our political differences drive us apart" was unable to dispel the suspicions that emerged as a result of this strange mix of women—independent feminists and members of the PAN, PRD, and PRI. What were these women plotting? *Proceso* magazine reflected this machista anxiety on its cover with a photo of Robles (PRD), Sahagún (PAN), and Elba Esther Gordillo (PRI) and the cover title *"El argüende."** The celebration of the vote on October 17 received a lot of media coverage, but the spotlight was focused on the three women on the cover of *Proceso*.

At the beginning of 2004, Rosario Robles, after having been interim governor, became president of the PRD and

---

* Translator's note: *Argüende* refers to a marked feminine activity—women gossiping and discussing frivolous topics without men in the vicinity. The cover implied that the meeting had been a frivolous gathering of women to gossip and scheme in a distinctly and dangerously feminine way.

was later involved in a political scandal, with a love affair on the side. The image of this woman, who had been a role model for leftist feminist politics, and possibly a PRD presidential candidate, collapses completely. Although various PRD leaders were supposedly associated with the corrupt activities, the target of greatest indignation was Robles. How could the president of a political party make deals involving money with a very suspicious character with whom she was in love? Much dirty laundry on all sides was aired in public. But Robles was further questioned for the way in which her personal life became entangled with her public responsibility. The stereotypically feminine remark "My heart won out over my head" was used against women politicians, supporting the logic that when a woman is successful, she is the exception to the rule, but when she fails, it is proof that all women are the same. Robles's fall and her tarnished image had a huge impact on a sector of feminist activists.

That same year, Amalia García (PRD) assumed the governorship of the state of Zacatecas after confronting the internal opposition of her party. The undeniable support of the people overwhelmed resistance from the PRD. This first PRD governor had a long history of connections with feminism and, a few months after taking office, she called for a meeting on "State Reforms from the Gender Perspective." Following the logic of "Taking a Step Forward" (*"avanzar un trecho"*), female politicians from the other political parties attended the meeting, including the minister of social development (PAN) and a number of prominent women writers. The support received through the presence of political and intellectual figures strengthened the "Taking a Step Forward" project. Feminist consciousness was more widespread, and what at one time had to be coaxed—the unity of women vis-à-vis concrete objectives—was now much easier.

One clear example of this was the announcement in 2005 of a course at the Simone de Beauvoir Leadership Institute designed for female congressional candidates from several political parties. Activists from PAN, PRI, PRD, and Alternativa attended the course, which was financed by Oxfam International and the parties themselves. The theme that united women from different political postures was the "gender perspective" in politics. The biases that for many years had kept PAN members and feminism apart began to crack. Finding common ground above and beyond their differences became urgent.

While both the positive and negative goings-on in the lives of women politicians occupy headlines, feminist groups debate their relationship with power and the way to influence politics. Although the need to participate in politics places some limits on the excessive subjectivism that characterizes feminist activism, the *mujeristas'* identitarian stance persists. And despite the high level of participation at the national level, some feminists continue to take refuge in small sectarian groups.

But, beyond personal options for participation and methods for either taking or refraining from political action, the movement's political impact may be seen now not only in the work of women politicians, but also in the lives of a great many women. Feminism as a movement organized in a multiplicity of ways has made indubitable gains: its discourse concerning the rights of women has become a kind of emotional, political, and intellectual education that allows women to stop feeling like they were victims. Feminist demands, such as that of women's "empowerment," have seeped into mainstream discourse. Beyond the usual agreements or disagreements and the rivalries within a particular political wing, the movement's general objectives have been quietly taken up all across the length and breadth of the country.

A Provisional Balance

Now, at the dawn of a new century, it is clear that one sector of the feminist movement has solidified its presence in three important ways: (a) the professionalization, through financing, of institutionalized groups that work on specific issues (health, education, violence) through political lobbying for their demands; (b) the academic and political legitimization of the gender perspective through the proliferation of study programs, courses, colloquia, publications, forums, and research, and (c) the promotion of a set of political interventions that consolidate agreements and coalitions and that strengthen a discourse on equity that takes many feminist concerns and aspirations into account. The balance is very positive, even though Mexican women still face the challenge of building a more structured and better organized movement: one that is able to position itself as a broader political influence in order to affect the government's public policy decisions; one that is able to make the parties seriously incorporate the gender perspective into their programs and to run more feminist candidates on their electoral tickets; one that is able to create public recognition of the role of *machismo* in social problems; one that is able to act in conjunction with artists, critics, and intellectuals to promote a cultural critique of sexism. The best-known feminist political goal has been the construction and dissemination of a discourse that impels everyday women to demand their rights. Spreading the notion that women have rights has been the most effective way to get women to confront sexism in their day-to-day lives.

In addition to the feminists' success getting their messages out to the public, another important achievement is that the demand for political autonomy has been made a part of the general context of progress toward democracy. The willingness of feminists to put together pacts and coalitions shows that reaching agreements does not mean losing autonomy or critical judgment, nor does it mean working jointly with any one political group. Feminism plays a key role in the construction of Mexican democracy, establishing priorities and reaching minimum agreements in order to create new ways for women and men to relate to each other, with equality as the central principle. Many feminists express this aspiration to combine their agendas in unionist and political domains and to demand transparency in the use of public resources. One well-publicized victory was the legal indictment of the fundamentalist group "National Pro-Life Committee" (*Comité Nacional Pro Vida"*) for improper use of a donation of thirty million pesos from the Mexican Health Ministry (*Secretaría de Salud*). A portion of the money, which had been designated for women's health centers, was used to purchase MontBlanc pens and G-strings for women. The careful work of feminist civic organizations and the existence of the Federal Institute for Access to Information (*Instituto Federal de Acceso a la Información*) permitted them to discover this misappropriation of funds. This type of work exerts a positive impact, allowing the general goals of the movement to reach the different states of the republic. The feminist influence is visible in the lives of a huge number of women. Thus, millions of Mexican women transform themselves from victims of machismo into gendered agents in a history still being written.

Nevertheless, a paradox remains. The great success of Mexican feminism is that, as Carlos Monsiváis has said, feminism's main principles have affected women's behavior;[39] nevertheless, feminists are not yet powerful voices in the world of politics. Without doubt, there is an increasing prominence of women politicians who consider themselves feminists. The feminist call to action has efficiently mobilized a group of notable women: writers; artists; government officials, and politicians. These women have responded en masse and speak out on critical cases: for example, the release of Claudia, a woman imprisoned for killing the man who attempted to rape her. She injured him, but he died several hours later due to lack of medical attention.[40] Also, these women spoke out in defense in the case of Paulina, a teenage rape survivor who was denied a legal abortion (to which she was entitled) by the director of a public hospital.[41] These nationally prominent cases show the ways that Mexican feminists have been able to articulate solidarity actions and muster broad social support.

The movement as such, the diverse groups that make it up, is still not a mandatory reference point or a stakeholder in Mexican realpolitik. There are various reasons. First, this has to do with the absence of an organized feminist force, the lack of which makes it less influential for the parties. The "grassroots" of the movement are working-class women who, at the same time, have their own particular interests depending on their political party or their involvement in other movements, such as the popular urban movement. Second, the "*mala fama*"* of feminists, as in the stereotypes of lesbians or abortionists, does not lead to huge numbers

---

* Translator's note: The most obvious translation of "*mala fama*" would be "bad reputation;" however, the term in Spanish connotes a distinct kind of reputation, namely a kind of sexual looseness, unnaturalness or depravity often linked to the feminine in overt and covert ways.

of supporters. In addition, there is the scant participation of young people. Unlike what occurred in the 1970s, when twenty-something, middle-class women entered the movement and organized themselves into small groups, there has been a serious generational crisis for quite some time. The notable absence of young women involved in feminism can be interpreted as resistance to organizational forms that they do not see as their own. But one should not underestimate the effect of the feminist movement's "*mala fama*." Despite the fact that many people and political organizations assume feminism theories, not all women accept a movement that is identified publicly with abortion and lesbianism. Many women who privately support feminist demands are unwilling to do so in public, because these go against the reigning paradigm of "normality" and "naturalness" with regard to what a women is and are in opposition to the Catholic dogmas so deeply entrenched in the society. Thus, the defense of sexual and reproductive rights taken up by the feminist movement hinders its acceptance into the national political arena. No political party wants to alienate the Catholic Church; in fact, the majority of politicians try to avoid making any commitments at all. Understood in this manner, the difficulties faced when trying to broaden the movement have a distinct cause, and, at least in part, explain the desire of a sector of the movement to build a new political configuration, a party, in which these demands can be raised without fear.

Although one cannot demand of the feminist movement what is still missing in other movements and political parties—a truly democratic operation or performance—one challenge that must be faced is that of confronting an "internal" difficulty. The different movement groups should recognize their difficulties and successes over the last few

years, should analyze what they have achieved and what
remains to be won, and should work together to formulate
a political agenda that connects the demands of each sector
of the movement and broadens these demands to embrace
the claims of the entire society. It is a fact that the subjective
dynamic of feminist activists hinders the movement's political development. Feminists fascinated by the demand for
equality or seduced by the glorification of difference develop
an extreme form of activism. The important goal for them is
not to achieve a political end, but rather, to share the feeling
of belonging, express their beliefs to the world, and enjoy the
unquestionable pleasure of the group relationship. For this
reason, it is essential to recognize something fundamental at
the cornerstone of all politics: subjectivity. Barcellona says
that the "space of the recovery of subjectivity is existence,
suffering, and life's pain that prevents us from saying 'I am
nothing,'"[42] thus, the need to say "I am something:" I am
woman; I am indigenous, I am gay. One task of the democratic project is to build a collective praxis that recognizes
particular identities and that is able to move beyond these
into a broader vision. To do this, we must understand how
the process of socialization and psychic introjection of cultural mandates is a determining factor in the construction
of some political identities. This awareness, plus the desire
for democracy, leads to an internal reformulation, in which
mujerista demands are slowly displaced, and instead of ideological posturing, political realities are seen as key.

Probably the most notable change in this sector of feminists interested in political action has been the desire to
articulate civic action in a different way. The "institutional"
feminists have attempted to reconcile their private motiva-
tions with public needs, and they have made great efforts
to acquire the basic political skills needed to develop a less

endogamous political practice. But increasing specialization and professionalization have introduced elements of unsuspected competition: critiques of elitism and university privilege are widespread, and populist and antiintellectual voices crop up again. The struggle against antiintellectual attitudes is a battle at the very heart of the movement. Nevertheless, increasingly, activists become more aware of how essential it is to work reflexively. Reflexivity is indispensable for strengthening democratic political identities. The generalized use of the phrase "gender perspective" is just one obvious example: this idea represents a conceptual leap in the explanation of women's subordination. This type of intellectual effort resonates with activists and gives rise to deeper analysis and the dissemination of knowledge.

Perhaps the main lesson learned by the feminist movement in these last thirty years or so is the absence of a natural bond that unites women: unity must be constructed politically. This has placed greater value on relationships with other political players and has driven many feminists to become involved in the more pragmatic side of political work. In addition to trying to exert influence on the electoral realm, there is an extraordinary interest from feminists around the country in building a common agenda and in developing mechanisms to influence the realpolitik. An emblematic case is that of Patricia Mercado who, despite several failed attempts, continues with her "right to insist" on the formation of a feminist political force. Her goal is to organize a political party, and, in 2005, she was able to reregister in order to compete in the 2006 federal election. This time, she will run under a different name, Alternativa, because election officials will not allow her to use the previous one. This tenacious desire to participate in realpolitik is a significant indicator of the transformation in this sector of the movement, which has been willing to move forward with a different collective praxis.

Due to these concrete advances, the possibility exists that many new feminists will leave identity politics in favor of a broader, civic focus. To do this, we will have to return to the critique of the materiality of social relations and question certain power structures more rigorously. This implies forging a praxis that unravels certain subjective necessities and that broadens the actual conceptualization of citizenship. Redefining the borders of civic action presupposes an interesting challenge for feminists: improving their position in the existing social order, while at the same time attempting to transform this order. However, perhaps creating processes that bring people together and achieving goals for the society at large could change the balance of institutional power. This could also transform contemporary political discourse and open politics to new identities that would be less selfish and self-centered and more altruistic and collaborative. Barcellona says that "democracy is a common grammar that underlies individual liberty."[43] Building new social connections, repairing the social fabric in a different, noncorporatist way, requires a different construction of a feminine "we" ("*nosotras*") that productively resolves the confrontation between a feminine "they" and a masculine "they" ("*ellas*" and "*ellos*"). This challenge, which reflects the tension between the recognition of diversity and surmounting it in a broader civic action, has become an urgent necessity for Mexican feminism.

To this end, the movement has begun gradually to accept the same diversity at its core and to understand that the existence of different tendencies and positions makes the movement stronger. In a *machista* society, feminism is radical by its very nature. Thus, the different strategic perspectives—from feminists willing to negotiate to the most intransigent ones—point in the same direction: ensuring that sexual difference is not translated into inequality. Unfortunately, identitarian reductionism gives rise to fragmentation. Only an internally critical process will lead to the construction of a political practice worthy of the name "feminist." Those of us who still defend the possibility of a leftist politics think a coalition of diversities is possible, but only if it renounces an exclusionary, essentialist, and identitarian method of protest and defends absolute respect for sexual and reproductive rights as a fundamental axis of democratic and republican politics. In this vision, the role of feminism, in all of its different forms, is essential.

CHAPTER 2

Equal Opportunity and Affirmative Action in the Workplace

The Theoretical Perspective for Approaching the Question

Elimination of discriminatory treatment against all groups is a requirement for a more equitable development of the entire society. Thus, it has become an urgent need for the government to design policies that take into account the cultural, economic, and sociopolitical determinants that produce discrimination against one half of the population. Antidiscriminatory measures can be understood as the set of normative, judicial, and communicative programs and solutions meant to remedy existing inequalities and to prevent their appearance in the future; any analysis of these measures must begin by explaining the framework to be used in considering the "problem" of women. This analysis implies both an examination of the concept of discrimination, as well as an understanding of the complexity of women's demands, which entails both the goal of equality and the recognition of difference.

To address the political vicissitudes faced during the establishment of rules and programs on women's and men's equality in the workplace, one must have a clear idea of the perspective to be employed in the formation of the actions. This is important not only because a fundamental element of public policy is an adequate theoretical framework, but also because such clarity aids in effective lobbying for antidiscriminatory action in the workplace.

In the process of devising measures to eliminate sexist discrimination, the main point of debate has been the appropriate position to take in regard to the unquestionable fact of sexual difference. At an international level, there are protective norms and positions (that recognize feminine specificity solely as types of disability or social minority), as well as enabling norms or positions (that are inspired by a conception of "complex equality" required to "enable" women). It is interesting that the boundary between "protective" and "enabling" legislation has not been rigid. Sociopolitical conditions have determined the level of effectiveness of one or the other.

In political theory on rights, equality means ignoring the differences between individuals for a specific purpose or within a particular context in order to support the excluded groups' demands for justice. Michael Walzer states it this way: "The root meaning of equality is negative; egalitarianism in its origins is abolitionist politics. It aims at eliminating, not all differences, but a particular set of differences, and a different set at different times and places."[1] This assumes a social agreement for considering obviously different people as (nonidentical) equals as a means to a particular end. With this usage, the opposite of equality is inequality or inequivalence, the noncommensurability of individuals or groups in certain circumstances for set purposes. Therefore, to qualify as a citizen, the requirement or "measure of equivalence" has been, variously, the following: independence (not a slave or servant); having property; being white; being a man; or being of a certain age. As a result of certain well-targeted battles, the notion of citizenship was gradually broadened to include nonproperty-owning men, blacks, and, finally, women. No one would consider women and men to be identical, but it is accepted that they are "equals" in terms of citizenship.

The political notion of equality includes—and in fact depends upon—recognition of the existence of difference. Arguments in support of demands for equality have usually been implicit or do not openly recognize difference. If groups or individuals were identical or equal, there would be no need to demand equality. This is the reason that this could be defined as a deliberate indifference to specific differences.[2]

Placing equality and difference in opposition to one other has a dual effect. First, this supposition ignores the fact that difference has figured in political notions of equality for quite some time; further, it suggests that similarity is the only basis for recognition of equality. This perspective puts women in an impossible position, because as long as the debate is confined to the terms of this oppositional discourse, one is forced to accept the conservative premise that since women cannot be identical to men, they cannot hope to achieve equality.[3]

The use of concepts of equality and difference in relation to women and men becomes extremely complex: both are equal as human beings, but different in terms of sex. This is why ways of thinking that opt, completely and without nuance, for either equality or for difference always end up being insufficient. Theoretical frameworks are needed that would allow us to articulate nonreductionist modes of thought about the issues faced by women. It is not enough to reify the old hierarchy set by gender in regard to sexual difference;

one must go further and recognize the impossibility of establishing the superiority of one sex over another. This assumes an acceptance of difference between women and men, while not translating this difference into inequality. Thus, public policies that try to "protect" difference end up strengthening it, and those that solely hope to achieve equality have largely been surpassed by proposals for equality in conjunction with a recognition of difference. To defend this perspective, one must pay a considerable amount of attention to the political context.[4] There are multiple political dimensions of the equality versus difference debate, especially in a period of conservative backlash such as the current one. One must be conscious of the very real danger that arguments about "women's natural difference" could be used to keep women in very limited roles and spaces.

In addition, the "dilemma of difference" must be understood.[5] This dilemma derives from the fact that, when dealing with subordinated groups, ignoring difference leads to flawed neutrality, but focusing on difference can accentuate the stigma of variation. Both in emphasizing and in ignoring difference, one runs the risk of recreating it. This is the dilemma, as formulated by legal scholar Martha Minow.[6]

When equality and difference are posited in dichotomy to each another, they establish an impossible choice. If a woman opts for equality, she will no longer be able to assert the demands that derive from her difference; however, if she opts solely for difference, she is admitting that equality is unattainable. Women cannot give up the claim to difference or to equality, at least in terms of our political system's principles and values. How could we recognize and utilize matters of sexual difference and argue for equality at the same time?

One possibility is to expose the construction that posits equality as the antithesis of difference. This leads to a rejection of the subsequent dichotomous constructions in political decision-making. The theoretical alternative is to reject the opposition of equality and difference and constantly to insist on equality *in* difference: "difference as the condition of individual and collective identities, as the continual challenge of recognizing these identities, history as the repeated illustration of the game of differences, differences as the real meaning of equality itself."[7]

At times, it makes sense for mothers to ask for their social role to be considered, while, in other contexts, maternity is irrelevant in assessing women's behavior. In some situations, it makes sense to ask that the value of what has been socially constructed as "woman's work" be reevaluated ("comparable worth" strategies are a contemporary example), while in other contexts, it is more important to prepare women to take on "nontraditional" jobs. What is unacceptable is to affirm that femininity predisposes women to do certain jobs (caretaking) or to have certain work styles (collaborative), since this posits as "natural" something that is actually a set of complex economic and social processes and, even worse, obscures the differences that have characterized women's labor histories.[8]

In terms of strategies for governmental policy, there must both be attention paid to the ways that difference operates, and an insistence on the existence of differences, but within the framework of an egalitarian vision. The resolution to the "dilemma of difference" does not ignore difference itself; rather, it entails a twofold, critical posture. The first aspect of this stance is the systematic criticism of the following schemes that utilize difference: the first distinguishes the diverse types of exclusions and inclusions—the hierarchies—constructed in the process. The second is a repudiation of the essentializing of difference; nonetheless, this is not a repudiation in the name of an equality that implies likeness or sameness. Rather, on the contrary it posits an equality constructed through differences. Sameness is not a requirement for equality. Women and men can be equal and yet not identical.

One of the crucial tasks is to clarify the differences that are produced socially: for example, the specific situation of women who have not worked due to domestic obligations or that of women who receive less pay in traditionally female jobs. Once these differences are identified, problems arise with respect to their conceptualization. The way one understands the apparent relationship between being woman and the inferiorization of the female sex will lead to a perspective that privileges either equality or difference. Those who think that the former is the same as the latter will seek to "deconstruct" the difference between the sexes, converting it into one of the many individual and social differences (in the plural). On the other hand, those who choose to "reconstruct" the social and symbolic order around sexual difference, decentering the idea of man with a capital "M," will distinguish the fact of being a woman from the inferiorization that the feminine sex suffers.[9]

It is very simplistic to reduce equality to plain equivalence, since the principle of equality is in itself an important factor in the normalization of differences. We need to think about equality starting with difference, without denying the existence of power relations between the sexes, since these are at the root of the debate about the status of women. The persistence of the power imbalance between the sexes is very serious; not even developed countries have been able to resolve it, even though there is greater equity at present. In these countries, subordination does not take the conspicuous form of discrimination, but rather hides itself behind the more sophisticated appearance of neutrality. True equity between women and men means reaching equality while recognizing difference.

The Predecessors of Affirmative Action

In the midst of the feminist resurgence of the 1970s, the first United Nations World Conference on Women was held in Mexico in 1975. The conference called for attention to the worldwide situation of subordination and discrimination against women. The majority of countries that signed the declaration emerging from the conference enacted laws and made reforms in their constitutions to guarantee equal rights and obligations for women. That year, the International Labor Organization adopted the Declaration and the UN Plan of Action (LX Meeting, 1975) and established a program to promote equality of opportunity and treatment for women workers, adopted by the International Labor Conference. Beginning at this time, the governments of numerous countries developed a series of programs, measures, regulations, and agreements for attaining workplace equality between men and women.

What was the strategy behind the actions taken on behalf of women? Did each nation find its own path, or did they follow a shared course of action to resolve the problem? What have been the most effective strategies? The most commonly faced problems? How have male and female workers responded? What about businesses and unions? To what extent is that model applicable in Mexico?

To answer these questions and to evaluate the alternatives proposed by other governments to combat workplace discrimination against women, it was critical to analyze the *corpus* of programs, measures, and governmental regulations of a number of European and North American countries. This material confirmed the existence of a set of clearly defined policies: equality of opportunity with clear guidelines for affirmative action.

In order to evaluate the viability of affirmative action in Mexico, it is essential to clarify the logic that led a substantial number of countries to move from policies based on equal treatment to equal opportunity policies and, finally, to promote affirmative action. Given that there has been a lack of available information in Mexico on arguments both for and against equality of treatment and opportunity, and even less on the debates concerning quotas and affirmative action, I have decided to explain the line of thinking behind this strategy. This is the principal strategy used at an international level to combat workplace discrimination against women. Thus, this chapter is rather than an enumeration of the steps or stages of the programs and more than a simple summary or classification of their experiences, I prioritize a reasoned explanation of the process that led various governments in developed countries to adopt this perspective. That is, I attempt to elucidate the political justification behind the examples I am studying, emphasizing the most common mechanisms used to set up equal opportunity programs, along with their risks and advantages.

For the last several years, under the auspices of the UN, nearly all governments worldwide designed programs to achieve equality of rights and obligations between women and men. The experiences of these countries that, in the mid-1980s, reviewed the effectiveness of sexual equality legislation enacted in 1975 are especially helpful. Many governments thought that implementation of certain legal measures to regulate social equality would lead to an erosion of inequality between women and men. However, a few years later, it became clear that an unequal society tends to replicate inequality in its institutions, even when equality may be legally or constitutionally guaranteed. After ascertaining the limited effectiveness of egalitarian policies, the issue of discrimination was found to be more complex than previously thought. In addition, the measures for achieving social and workplace equality had no significant effects if family life was not restructured concurrently and if advantageous conditions for women were not established.

The core of the lesson was that it was not sufficient to declare equality of treatment, when equality of opportunity did not exist. This means, for example, that even when there is clear discrimination in the workplace, its origins are found outside of that space. The different roles played by women and men in the home and the consequences of this gender assignment in daily life hinder the progress of any proposal for equality. Equal treatment for socially unequal individuals does not result per se in equality.

In 1983, the Norwegian government stated that it was impossible to achieve equality of social status between women and men by simply prohibiting discriminatory treatment; if one wishes to remedy this disparity in the contemporary world, it is critical to provide women with an advantage in certain fields. Thus, a set of measures meant to remedy the disparity in social treatment between women and men has been formulated within equal opportunity programs. These programs have been called affirmative action or positive action programs. The UN argues that the adoption of special, temporary measures designed to accelerate actual equality between women and men can never be considered a discriminatory act against men.

Throughout this entire process, justice has been the main concern of both the UN and of governments. The essence of justice is equal treatment for those who are equal or equivalent (this is not to say identical). In this way, the particular conceptualization of equality will lead to a decision to either defend or oppose these steps to improve the status of women.

The level of interest in justice is basically conditioned by political ideology: this is what determines governmental positions on antidiscriminatory actions. Therefore, conservative governments do not promote affirmative action in the same way as liberal or progressive governments do.

For European Union countries, affirmative action has created equality of opportunities more effectively than other programs, not only because affirmative action leads to balance between the sexes, but also because it creates a more just society. In fact, the most advanced Western democracies have designed innovative projects to attract, promote, and retain greater numbers of women in the workplace. These countries have proposed going even further than affirmative action, without abandoning it completely based on the principle of recognizing and capitalizing on diversity in the workplace.

The future of affirmative action seems to be an equitable administration of diversity. The awareness generated by affirmative action, first with regard to black people and later in regard to women, is useful for understanding and unraveling certain cultural codes. Thus, prejudices and stereotypes can be exposed and combated more effectively. The context that conditions the reception of affirmative actions has gradually shifted. More than a concession or a favor, affirmative action is now perceived as a mechanism for social change that benefits everyone. Some companies recognize that they pursue these policies because it is in their interest, since they benefit the company as a whole.

In addition, affirmative action is a policy that contains the seeds of its own demise. Affirmative action will no longer be needed when equality of opportunity is achieved, when the critical role of gender is recognized, when nonsexist education is a reality, when cultural patterns are more egalitarian. This is already occurring in a number of places, as in Scandinavian countries that are beginning to formulate policies of "gender neutrality." This means that to deal with discrimination there is no distinction between men and women, but instead, discrimination is dealt with when it is intentional.

Sexual Discrimination and Gender

When the UN developed its convention on the elimination of all forms of discrimination *against women*, which was formally announced in New York on December 18, 1979, the same conception of discrimination used by the International Convention on the Elimination of All Forms of Racial Discrimination (New York, March 7, 1966) was employed. It is not surprising that Article 1 of each is the same in both documents, since all antidiscrimination programs are based on the basic UN definition of discrimination:

> For the purposes of the present Convention, the term "discrimination against women" shall mean any distinction, exclusion or restriction made on the basis of sex which has the effect or purpose of impairing or nullifying the recognition, enjoyment or exercise by women, irrespective of their marital status, on a basis of equality of men and women, of human rights and fundamental freedoms in the political, economic, social, cultural, civil or any other field.[10]

As racial and sexual discrimination are commensurable to a certain extent, the corresponding measures to alleviate them have taken parallel tracks. However, this shared starting point made it necessary to refine the conceptual definition of discrimination according to sex, since it becomes possible to construct an effective model for intervention only after precisely identifying what is to be combated and remedied.

When dealing with sexism or discrimination based on gender, one confronts situations not faced with other types of discrimination. For example, racism in the workplace is very obviously discrimination, because it is absurd to take the color of someone's skin into account when looking at work performance. However, in the case of women, there are cultural presumptions that have persisted over the course of history regarding women's physical weakness, their vulnerability during pregnancy, or their special role (conceived of as irreplaceable) within a certain model of family. According to these conceptions, it is fully "justified" to "protect" women from certain jobs, although this manner of treating women conceals or produces discrimination. The structure of society itself is based on these assumptions that, over the years, have clearly become prejudices. In this way, certain jobs become "niches" within which women are supposedly "protected," although really they are trapped.

It is therefore crucial to understand that discrimination against women is produced both on an individual and collective basis, both deliberately and unconsciously, since it is interwoven with customs and tradition. In this way, it is made visible both through direct attacks on their interests or on women themselves, and through indirect attacks, as a result of the operation of the social system or in the application of seemingly neutral measures that have specific repercussions for women. This is due to the fact that women are in less of a position to deal with their effects, or because some of their characteristics concentrate the negative effects of a certain activity on them. All of this means that women, as a result of their gendered social position, face barriers that prevent them from full participation in the societies in which they live.

One premise of antidiscriminatory action is recognizing that culture uses gender to introduce discrimination on the basis of sex. Taking the anatomy of women and men and their obviously different reproductive functions as a point of reference, each culture establishes a set of practices, ideas, discourses, and social representations that attribute differential characteristics to them. This symbolic construction, which in social science is termed *gender*, regulates and conditions people's subjective and objective behavior; that is, through the process of the construction of gender, society produces the ideas of what women and men should be and of what is assumed to be "inherent" in each sex.

Thus, workplace inequalities cannot be rectified if one is not aware of the social presuppositions that have been barriers to equality, especially the effects generated by the division between the private (feminine) and the public (masculine) spheres. The enduring condition of women's marginalization, their typical departure from the workplace during essential years of their lives, the lesser value attributed to feminine jobs, their insufficient professional training, the introduction of a sole model of femininity, and the fact that, in many cases, women themselves do not recognize their status as victims of discrimination, mean that we need a politics that recognizes the existence of past injustice, its persistence, and the complicity of its own victims in its perpetuation. The situation cannot be changed by simply responding with a set of legal guidelines that establish equality between women and men; what are needed are proactive, affirmative actions that rectify the persistent, subtle, and hidden factors that put women at a disadvantage in comparison with men, and cause that those who evaluate and hire them doubt their work abilities.

Given that one principle of antidiscriminatory action is recognition that sexism is a cultural attitude resulting from a certain history, in order to detect sexism and to evaluate its extent, it is crucial to understand the societal context surrounding the women who would benefit from the program. In addition, since discrimination has many facets, it is critical to begin with a diversity of measures, of a real program to intervene in distinct social spheres. Some components of sexism can be dealt with separately, as long as one does not lose sight of the whole in developing a comprehensive plan. This comprehensiveness is a fundamental principle of antidiscriminatory action.

Equality of Treatment or Equality of Opportunity?

In regard to sexist discrimination, Western democracies have reached the conclusion that there is no greater injustice than providing equal treatment to people in such different situations as those of women and men. The main point is that treating people as equals does not mean providing equal treatment. An example: if a company decided to buy same-size uniforms for all of its employees, they would be giving what one assumes to be equal treatment, although the results would be unequal: not all women would fit into the uniform. In the same way that this company does not provide equal treatment—even though they apparently offer the same thing to all the female employees—a company in which there is sexual harassment or where there is no childcare service is not treating its male and female employees equally.

In the end, equitable treatment is insufficient, since not all people have had the same opportunities for receiving an education or workplace training. Thus, there is a turn toward the idea of promoting "equality of opportunity." At the basis of this proposal is the idea that if people are offered the same opportunities, they will be able to get ahead through their own work and effort. But, if "equality of opportunity" is not supported with proactive measures, there is a risk that if someone does not achieve equality, this person would be held responsible, as if it were a personal failure. Therefore, the implementation of affirmative actions is absolutely necessary, because what appear to be personal circumstances are often the result of unrecognized structural issues, such as gender. An equal opportunity policy that does not include affirmative action operates as if what matters were the intent, and this puts too much faith in the will of the individual. On the other hand, a policy that includes affirmative actions starts with the idea that good intentions are not sufficient to deal with the unjust framework established years ago; therefore, additional efforts are required.

It is interesting to recall the experience of the United States, where the first laws on affirmative action were enacted in 1964. Neither the law nor the Equal Employment Opportunity Commission (EEOC) mentioned sex specifically; they spoke only of race, color, religion, or national origin. Later, an amendment related to sex was introduced. This amendment employed the phrase "affirmative action," which the Labor Department defined as the development of policies that would guarantee equal opportunity in the workplace through internal monitoring to identify problem areas and through development of specific actions to prevent inequality. The low hiring levels of a minority group had to be resolved by setting goals to raise the representation of this group and by establishing a timetable for achieving these goals.

These programs were designed to combat intentional discrimination: for example, discrimination in offices where no black people were being hired. Although initial affirmative action plans were based on cases of illegal discrimination at several companies, more general measures were established later. For example, the federal government would not contract companies that did not do everything possible to increase the number of minority group members from historically underrepresented groups.

Initially, the explicit criteria of the United States were the following:

1. The purpose of affirmative action plans should be to break with the old patterns of segregation and hierarchy and to establish access to work opportunities that are traditionally closed.
2. Other employees should not be fired, and there should be no new barriers to their development.
3. The plan must be temporary, intended to eliminate an imbalance.

The US experience is important because of the concept that affirmative action should not only deal with compensating specific people for past wrongdoing and injustice, but also should attempt to redistribute jobs, promotions, and positions in a more equitable manner among the different groups in society.

Given the entrenched sexism in the workplace, an equal opportunity policy that includes affirmative action is perceived as more effective, because simply declaring that a person's sex should not be used as the basis for discrimination does not erase the brutal reality. Affirmative action forces a consciousness of the workings of gender, not because these are the most important things for consideration when evaluating a worker, but because ignorance of the differences that gender produces leads to a false homogeneity, in which it is implicitly presupposed that all workers are men. It is crucial to note that the aim of these actions is not to "correct" one half of the population for their "inadequacy" due to their sexual difference, but rather, to make amends and adjustments to a system that treats people unequally.

Furthermore, while making these adjustments, one cannot conceive man as the sole referent, with woman in opposition to him as the "other," the different, or the strange. Moreover, it is essential to question certain ideas and norms set by gender which appear "natural" to us, but that are socially constructed. Taking into account extraeconomic and cultural factors in relation to workplace decisions is the decisive element for these programs to be successful.

Equal Opportunity Programs in the Workplace: The Rejection of Quotas and the Acceptance of Affirmative Action

Equal opportunity programs were first put in place in the workplace, since there was an urgent priority to eliminate discrimination, due to its overwhelming impact on women. At the beginning, it was assumed that if both sexes were treated equally, sexist discrimination would disappear: if women had the jobs, they would do the work the same as men, move up the ladder like them, and would even have identical needs. Because women in all countries are in a disadvantaged position in the workplace, the thinking was that it was simply a question of offering women the same work opportunities as men.

The first thing that became clear was that women's cultural upbringing—teaching girls and young women to be "feminine"—is also job training that prepares them for certain kinds of work. In the labor market, there is a constant need for workers in many positions categorized as "feminine," which are an extension of domestic labor and the care that women provide for children and adults. There are also characteristics considered "feminine" that are valued in the workplace, such as attention to detail and a submissive attitude. Although this "masculine-feminine" categorization is disappearing in many highly developed countries and there are increasingly many women who do nontraditional jobs (carpenters, electricians, mechanics, etc.), in European countries with Mediterranean cultures (Spain, Italy, Greece), there is not yet a large and steady supply of women aspiring to male-identified jobs. Obviously, the situation is even worse in Islamic countries and in Latin America. However, this is a growing trend, because it is easier for women to enter "masculine" jobs than for men to work in "feminine" jobs that usually tend to be more poorly paid, although cultural and psychological factors also weight heavily as, for example, doing work considered feminine is interpreted as undermining a man's virility.

Inequality is also expressed in terms of salaries: women earn much less than men. The existing division between "feminine" and "masculine" jobs precludes an argument based on the principle of "equal salary for equal work." The segregation of the workforce prevents women from entering better-paying and more prestigious jobs. In all types of organizations, women are in an unequal situation; they are rarely found in high management or directorial positions. Sexual harassment and intimidation are an unfortunate reality in the workplace. Although there are increasingly higher numbers of women in high-level technical and scientific positions and in important posts in politics and public administration, women continue to represent a small percentage in these fields. Subtle discrimination at high levels is not recognized, nor are the invisible barriers of the "glass ceiling," a term employed to describe the imperceptible obstacles that prevent women from reaching directorial positions. This invisible hurdle is twofold: both the barriers (the "ceiling") that women internally impose on their aspirations and the hidden mechanisms used by organizations to keep women from being promoted.

The undervaluing of women's paid labor is connected with the invisibility of both housework and care giving for others. Women's unpaid work is tightly intertwined with their paid work. How women enter the formal or informal labor market is linked with how they handle or resolve their work in the home. The consequences of the entwining of housework with remunerated labor include the physical and emotional burden of the double workday, a brutal limitation on women's opportunities for personal development, political participation as citizens, and emotional and social lives. An added effect is the workplace vulnerability implied in missing work in order to take care of a domestic or familial problem.

Historically, domestic labor has not been recognized as real work, partly because of the idea that care giving for people in the private realm is an expression of love, and also because of the way that work has been traditionally defined as a paid activity. Domestic labor performed by women within the family and working women's confinement to the low-paid, female ghetto are complementary aspects of the same problem, as are sexual harassment, low salaries, and the devaluing of women's capacities in the labor market. All of these elements are structurally linked. In fact, all of the aspects of women's workplace situation are interrelated: occupational segregation; pay discrimination; sexual harassment; and an overwhelming work load caused by familial demands and the lack of social services.

In addition, the great majority of women share the same assessments of value that lead to their discrimination. This phenomenon is "symbolic violence," that is, violence that is exercised against a social agent with their complicity or consent.[11] Thus, when women attempt to work in other arenas, they reproduce attitudes that reinforce their traditional image as incapable of performing certain jobs. This fact, combined with the lack of support that could ease the load of the domestic and familial obligations assigned to women, makes working outside the home extremely costly on a personal level for women. It is common for many female workers to say that they miss the traditional, idealized role of the protected housewife provided for by her husband, although that role also has its costs. The existence of this conflict is used to confirm that women "prefer" being at home to working.

Affirmative action began with the premise that it was essential to identify and eliminate the very real discrimination of working women in order to increase their presence in the workplace, to ensure their entrance into all occupations (even traditionally masculine fields), and to promote their career and professional development, providing the possibility of access to all jobs at all levels. Its initial objectives were the following: reduce the segregation of women that kept them working low level jobs with little social prestige and meager salaries; redistribute familial responsibilities; end sexual harassment; encourage the growth of women's presence in the world of work; and lay the groundwork for women to attain substantial professional advancement. In order for an affirmative action program to achieve concrete results, it must make changes to the company's system of priorities, internal organizational structure, and the behavior of the individuals involved. This restructuring of labor requires the development of new hiring policies and the creation of selection systems that guarantee job access to a fixed number of women. This number is set proportionally to the number of trained women workers and implies setting explicit goals for the percentages of women that should occupy certain positions. Also, it is crucial to reassess the economic value of so-called feminine jobs through salary modifications or through "comparable worth." The "comparable worth" strategy entails allocating a high wage value to "feminine" jobs that have no "masculine" equivalent by comparing the need that the company or the boss has for them. This assumes a substantial change in the perspective used to evaluate the job. Since there is neither equal access to different jobs nor wage equity between masculine and feminine jobs, "comparable worth" provides a way to break this vicious cycle.[12] It no longer demands "equal pay for equal work," but rather, "equal pay for work of equal value."

This reassessment also implies building alternatives, such as the creation of different promotion ladders in certain work settings so that women can apply their experiences and knowledge. For example, when a hospital has an opening for a nurse supervisor, it is not right for an administrative person with no experience caring for sick patients to be promoted to the job, while nurses with many years of experience are not allowed to compete, solely because they lack previous experience in administration (even though this issue could be alleviated in a few months with training).

Last but not least, affirmative action in the workplace requires a process of communication both to sustain it and to arrive at the real root of discrimination: the family. What is critical is to develop a new way of conceptualizing familial responsibilities, to find a new method for distributing work, and to create collective services, especially day care for small children. Antidiscriminatory action is based on education and on social communication. The formulation of large-scale policies in both fields is an effective instrument for changing customs and stereotypes.

Even though some plans for affirmative action have been questioned or reformulated, these policies play an undeniable role in driving and sustaining a move in society toward equality. Part of the resistance to affirmative action involves a type of confusion or misinformation. An important factor that leads to this misunderstanding is equating affirmative action with quotas or preferential treatment. Some have argued that workers as a group should not be blamed or have to pay through reparative measures for the injustices committed by society over centuries against a particular race or sex. However, affirmative actions should not be interpreted solely as reparations for damages, but rather fundamentally as the establishment of equitable conditions within a discriminatory context.

When defining criteria for employee selection, the US Department of Labor and Justice, the Equal Employment Opportunity Commission, and the Civil Service Commission referred to two necessary elements of an effective affirmative action program. The first is a study of the employee workforce to determine whether the percentages of race, sex, and ethnicity in the different workplace categories correspond to the percentages in the workforce supply. This means, for example, that the percentage of Mexican-American managers should be defined by taking into consideration both the percentage of the Mexican-American population at large and the percentage qualified for management work. The attempt to eliminate inequality should be structured by a demographic ratio: the percentages of workers employed should correlate to the workforce supply.

The second requirement states that if demographic inequality is found, all phases of the process of employee selection must be evaluated. Once the source of the exclusion is identified, affirmative action should be used to remedy it. Affirmative action should develop strategies for directed recruitment, workplace training, and skill building, validation of selection procedures, as well as other efforts to guarantee that candidates from minority groups are identified through appropriate criteria in matters related to hiring and promotion, and that these individuals be offered special training.

The American Association of University Professors (AAUP) formulated guidelines for implementing affirmative action in academia using these criteria. The first recommendation of the AAUP was that universities review their current policies to see whether they did or did not have a discriminatory or exclusionary impact. The AAUP argued that it was essential to analyze the criteria for staff hiring and selection in order to uncover the prejudices and assumptions of the individuals who establish them. Even policies that appear "neutral" can be problematic. Such is the case with rules against nepotism, which posit that one cannot hire both members of a couple; because women tend to be the younger halves of the couple, they are the ones who are not hired. In addition, the AAUP is against quotas and they make the case for their opposition utilizing the following example: if the proportion of women who have studied astrophysics is less than that of women who study literature, the correct proportion of female professors of astrophysics should be less than that of female professors of literature. This shows that a "general quota for women" should not be established, since the fact that there are fewer female professors of astrophysics does not necessarily mean discrimination exists, because the difference stems from the relative number of qualified women and the number of positions.

Although affirmative action programs differ from country to country and from one organization to another, they have certain general characteristics in common:

(a) A good affirmative action program is designed with goals specific to the composition of the workforce, establishing reasonable dates for reaching the correct percentages. For example, a company could decide that, depending on the number of women qualified for being managers in the workforce supply, one-third of mid-level managers should be women. Then, the company designs a plan to have 20% women in five years, 25% women in ten years, and 33% in fifteen years. Nevertheless, because there could be variations depending on changes in supply, what matters is not the exact quota, but rather the attempt to achieve a proportional relationship between the supply of women looking for work and the available positions.

(b) A good affirmative action program standardizes and regulates the process of staff recruitment in order to compensate for the defects in selection procedures; left unaddressed, these would generate an insufficient proportion of work for certain groups. Instead of a selection made by a single individual with their own set of prejudices or a traditionalist outlook on gender, a process could be based on impersonal mechanisms. In addition, it could incorporate the use of an additional factor (belonging to a certain group or sex), for example, in the case of an individual who was one of the three best candidates for a particular job. This factor could be the basis for a decision in their favor.

(c) Effective affirmative action programs establish certain special training procedures to correct potential employees' uneven levels of previous training. These training programs are especially useful for members of groups that are represented unequally and who have been unable to acquire the necessary job skills due to lack of opportunities and not personal incompetence. One notable example is "Bridges" in Canada, which identifies training needs, designs special programs, trains women, and puts them in contact with jobs that require these work skills.

(d) Good affirmative action programs guarantee equal pay for work of equal value. The job does not have to be identical to another in order to receive the same salary; rather, it must simply be of the same value to the company. In other words, it means accepting the mechanism of "comparable worth." Canada has indicated that some "neutral" formula must be applied to gender to evaluate the four factors that should be considered to measure a job's value: (1) skill; (2) effort; (3) responsibility required in on-the-job performance, and (4) the conditions under which the job is performed.

(e) Solid affirmative action programs recognize that there are "hidden" factors of discrimination and propose eliminating them. For example, they propose that childcare is a responsibility of both working parents, and seek joint solutions with the company, the community, and the government. By recognizing childcare as a political, economic, and social issue of great importance, its cost is redefined and resources are directed toward developing programs and services. In addition, the positive effects of sharing household responsibilities with men are a significant secondary benefit.

(f) Comprehensive affirmative action programs work with both employers and employees. The educational process of both groups is of the utmost importance. Much more than a simple talk is necessary. In Italy, workshops that include personal reflections have been very productive for male workers, bosses, and employers to gain an understanding of the cultural problems surrounding gender issues. In Canada, the pay equity program includes seminars, publications, self-help manuals, and counseling for employers, unions, and employees.

(g) Successful affirmative action programs have included campaigns to raise awareness and educate both the population in general and employers and workers in particular. This has been especially important in countries where gender-based stereotypes remain strong.

It is clear that a governmental agency is needed to observe, supervise, evaluate, or discipline companies to ensure that they abide by the legal guidelines. This has occurred in places where affirmative action has been legally mandated; such is the case of some European countries, Canada and the United States. When affirmative action is voluntary, governments establish fiscal incentives to encourage companies to develop programs.

The purview of the supervising agency can be general, such as that of the Equal Employment Opportunity Commission, which ensures that there is no workplace discrimination due to a number of different causes (race, sex, ethnicity or religious identification). Alternately, the purview can be specific, as in the case of the Office on Women in several Labor Departments.

Experiences of Selected Countries

Recent years have witnessed both a valuable process of improvement and redefinition of antidiscriminatory measures, as well as a restructuring of the programs designed to confront discrimination. The majority of the European democracies, particularly The Netherlands and the Nordic countries (Sweden, Denmark, Norway), have the most experience with this type of program. The United States has a rich history of affirmative action in relation to racial, ethnic, and national minorities that began in the 1970s. The perspective of Canada, whose law of workplace equity is one of the best (1994), draws on the experiences of many countries and combines these with its own particular cultural dynamic, that is, its dual Anglo- and Francophone population.

The majority of information provided by governmental agencies has to do with the reasons behind affirmative action and describes its programs. Both plans for bringing about equality between the sexes and descriptions of action programs are essentially the same, and brief reading shows how similar they are ad nauseam. Unfortunately, governmental information tends to be very program-descriptive, emphasizing achievements and minimizing problems. Thus, it has been necessary to analyze the experiences presented in the scant critical and evaluative information from academia in an attempt to understand what makes certain affirmative action programs more effective than others. In certain organizations, the programs show their effects rapidly; in others, progress is slow. There are companies that have had to confront worker resentment, while others are apparently free of this phenomenon. What are the elements of a program that lead to its success? Where is the most resistance found?

After reading the material available, two constants become clear: (1) men's resentment and anger in the face of the invasion of women and (2) the resistance of women themselves to receiving "preferential treatment."

Some studies point out that management's commitment and staff receptivity (both crucial for the company and the union) are the two factors that determine success. Management's committed leadership (both in the public and private sector) is the variable that can predict the success of affirmative action programs. Certain essays posit that, in order to achieve success, this commitment must radiate from above; other essays state that this must come from below. Both point to the same goal: involvement of the entire organization. In the governmental documents reviewed, what is emphasized is the need to build awareness and to inform company directors, administrators, and key staff members about the goal of affirmative action, because the more people understand the overall goal, the more support they will assuredly provide. Unions that have participated in the process argue for the importance of building awareness in this way.

In order to prevent resistance to affirmative action, experience suggests that is crucial to provide an adequate explanation of what it is and what its different programs entail.

Not paying attention to the way the program is explained creates resentments. For example, it is one thing to say, "we have to follow a law the government has imposed on us and hire more women." It is a very different thing to bring up the issue in a more subtle way, helping men to see the benefits that will be obtained in the long term with this type of policy, from specific gains such as paternity leave to more general ones such as greater productivity. Appealing to a common good and not to the workers' personal interest will make them more likely to give their approval. The goal is to convince the key people—the natural leaders of the workers and bosses—that the entire society pays the price of discrimination against women, and that men will also pay over the long term through their daughters and granddaughters.

However, in some workplaces, the formation of an outreach group is imperative to build awareness among the workers and the administration. The process of internal reflection can cause great fear and vulnerability in relation to masculinity. Mishandling of these processes will only reaffirm *machismo*.

In order for affirmative action programs to be well received, it is critical that these programs take people's qualifications into consideration. The program is not about establishing quotas for women, because quotas provoke resentment and are interpreted as a means of giving preference to people who lack the necessary qualifications to carry out a job. In all cases, a careful evaluation of skills can help to select a woman who, with training, will end up performing as well as a man. Here one must distinguish between two types of programs: programs designed to increase women's access to certain jobs, and those that give women preference in hiring over equally qualified men. When men know that there is an affirmative action program in existence, they think that the women who are hired are less qualified than they. This is why it is important to stress that affirmative action gives preference to women only when dealing with equally qualified individuals; however, performance level must continue to be a crucial factor in the selection process.

Although it is necessary to convince male workers of the need for the good of affirmative action programs, it is even more urgent for women to accept them. A contradictory element of this type of program lies in the insistence by some of its female beneficiaries that they do not need affirmative action. For some, entering a job through this type of program diminishes their personal merit. This way of thinking arises both out of confusion between quotas and affirmative action, and also out of an individualistic approach, defined by an attitude of self-improvement that rejects the victimism of a *mujerista* discourse.

In the United States, which has the longest history with affirmative action of any nation, there is a growing phenomenon of people who feel less motivated when they obtain a job by means of quotas. Although conservative propaganda has undoubtedly increased attention regarding these cases, they are interesting because of what they signify. The publicized cases are about people who have entered the workplace due to a preference for their race or ethnicity. This situation has meant that, at many job sites, applicants are asked whether they would like to be considered for the position using affirmative action or not. Notwithstanding this, there is not a significant number of women who show signs of low self-esteem due to affirmative action. It is difficult to decide which choice is the lesser of two evils: having low self-esteem after getting a job thanks to being a woman, or not having a job, which also would reduce self-esteem. On the other hand, it has been proven that, when beneficiaries of affirmative action receive an explanation of how the selection was made, their self-esteem is not likely to be affected negatively. Getting a job through affirmative action does not mean a lack of merit. Additionally, in order to remain in a job, one must be extremely dedicated, and one must show, according to the evaluative standards of each company, that one has the skills necessary to perform the job.

The central problem lies in the difficulty of knowing how a specific person or group of people will handle difference. There are people who, conscious of the existence of prejudice, go to the other extreme and overvalue the achievements of people from discriminated groups. On the other hand, others do not even think about this issue and allow their prejudices to take hold. Walter Massey, a black scientist, said that the difficult part of being black is never knowing how good you really are. As he explained, if you do not achieve what you want, you can think that it is because of racial prejudice or discrimination; however, if you do achieve it, then you have a sneaking suspicion that it is because of affirmative action.

Nonetheless, in certain work arenas like in public administration or upper-level management, women themselves are beginning to reject affirmative action, because it carries with it a stigma regarding the apparent lack of personal skill. Undoubtedly, the vehemence with which certain women attack affirmative action is due in part to a defensive attitude and to their being self-referential: they believe that any success that they accrue is due only to their efforts and talent. They do not have an awareness of other women's experiences. In fact, their rejection or discomfort also stems from the condescension that is typically apparent when dealing with the beneficiaries of affirmative action. There is a concern among women that excessive attention to their sex diminishes their own personal achievements, leading many to refuse affirmative action and opt to compete with men with no special treatment or favoritism.

The majority of governments recognize that the positive part of some programs lies in that they cause the majority of workers to reflect upon themselves and their own behavior. The more that the cultural division between public and private is questioned and companies offer broadened familial supports, another type of emotional or affective benefit appears, because men have more time available to spend on family issues and can be in greater contact with their children.

Notwithstanding this scenario, this analysis should not end on an overly optimistic note. Although personal interest can influence some men's attitudes toward affirmative action, one should not forget that the bulk of resistance often hides certain kinds of hostility or contempt, that are produced by misogyny or *machismo*. Studies show that the obstacle hindering affirmative action the most is either racism or sexism. However, when existing prejudices against women or ethnic groups are more widely recognized, the problem can be sorted out and strategies can be designed to combat resistance.

A recent phenomenon is men speaking out about injustices done to them by affirmative action programs. More than twenty years went by after the implementation of the law in the United States before a man brought a legal suit against an affirmative action plan. Although this person alleged that a less competent woman was hired, because the rating he received was two points higher, the court decided that sex could be considered as a decisive factor in hiring because there was an obvious imbalance in the percentage of women in certain work categories in relation to the percentage of women in the local workforce.

To summarize, the negative aspects of affirmative action can be mitigated by educating all those who would benefit, directly or indirectly, about the general usefulness of this type of action. To this end, it is essential to implement feedback mechanisms in the workplace, as well as instituting campaigns focused on undoing cultural prejudices. Education is affirmative action's greatest ally. Therefore, both in schools and through the mass media, sustained educational support is critical. Social communication is the perfect tool for informing and educating the public on the mass cultural change brought about by more women in the workplace: transformation in the role of the family, domestic habits, and social traditions.

Conclusion: Equity Is Good for Everyone

It is one thing to say that affirmative action is necessary and fair, and it is another to measure its effectiveness. How much can it achieve? It ends up being difficult to separate the effects of a particular policy from the effects of general social and economic change: how responsible are modernizing trends and cultural change for transformation in women's work situation? Although it is ultimately difficult to separate the influences caused by general social transformations from those caused by affirmative action programs, the available evidence suggests the importance of affirmative action on influencing the direction of change.

A gauge for evaluating the effects of antidiscriminatory measures is determining the extent to which the original objectives have been achieved. The goal of affirmative action is to replace the illusion of equality based on the idea of equal treatment with real equality of opportunities. If we analyze trends in developed nations that have implemented affirmative action, we find that, even when asymmetries persist, the size of the gap has been reduced, a decrease measured both by a smaller wage gap and by the higher number of women in nontraditional jobs or high-level positions.

However, it would not be right to evaluate the success of certain specific affirmative action programs solely with quantitative tools. Qualitative measurement of effectiveness is essential, because a good plan does not eliminate the disparities between women and men with the stroke of a pen. Rather, it initially attempts to help women to overcome victimization and the stigma of feeling personally responsible for their disadvantaged position, permitting them to recognize discrimination and to visualize the possibility of transforming their situation.

On the other hand, the fact that affirmative action has positive effects does not mean that all programs work perfectly. After reviewing the results of the programs, one can conclude that in places where affirmative action had limited effects, it has been due to the slow program implementation and to a lack of resources. One issue that appears to be one of the most serious in some countries is the government's inability to respond to complaints. For example, in the United States since the law was enacted, complaints made to the Equal Opportunity Commission (EEOC) show that workplace discrimination is far from disappearing. In 1985, there were 72,000 complaints, and the EEOC only filed suit in 411 cases. In 1990, there were 524 lawsuits, but 45,000 cases were left uninvestigated. The criticism and suggestions indicate that, to enforce the law, the institution in charge of monitoring the effective equality of workplace opportunities and treatment should be strengthened economically, and their array of disciplinary options should be broadened.

Among the positive changes stemming from affirmative action are those brought about by the simple fact of hiring women. Their ample presence in the labor market leads to a valuable differentiation in resources. Moving beyond the typical model of the male worker provides the company with a wider set of competencies. Feminine preferences and styles can lead to new ways of doing things: a nontraditional approach to problems, a willingness to reexamine which solutions work best. Women consistently produce changes that benefit all workers. For example, in Italy, the entry of female carpenters into a company led to a reduction in the number of carpenters with back injuries. The reason? It has to do with gender. Women began to ask for help carrying heavy boards, leading to a work style in which it was acceptable to ask for help. Previously, the male carpenters were embarrassed to admit that they were unable to carry something heavy by themselves, and they injured their backs in the process.

In addition, there is the symbolic aspect, which is very important for cultural change. The presence of a woman in a certain workplace does not only increase the organization's diversity; their presence also serves as an example for other women, especially young women, and contributes to breaking stereotypes that certain jobs are masculine.

The most important element of job equity is that women are not the only ones to benefit; job equity is also in the interest of men, minority groups, and the disabled. Promoting equity on the job means creating workplaces that reflect a society's plurality. In Canada, the categorization of groups assisted by its Employment Equity (*Équité en matière d'emploi*) is very interesting. There are four groups: (1) women; (2) indigenous peoples; (3) disabled people, and (4) members of visible minorities. The Royal Commission on

Equality in Employment explained clearly that it is not that the people in these four groups are inherently incapable of achieving equality themselves, but rather that the obstacles that they face are so formidable and self-perpetuating that they cannot be overcome without intervention. It is intolerable and insensitive to wait for the barriers to disappear over time. Equality in the workplace will not be achieved unless it is actively promoted.

It is also useful to speak out about certain problems, such as blindness to sexism. Imagining that everyone has the same life opportunities reflects a level of disinformation that renders it acceptable to blame the victim. It is essential to reeducate people in many aspects, but above all, in one essential way: recognition of and respect for difference. This entails a variety of things: from learning to work with people who are different to recognizing that difference is not solely a discrimination issue, but also, that difference has positive characteristics as well, such as different learning and administrative styles, different requirements for job satisfaction and different ways for people to develop their potential. Companies that do not deal with these issues can lose their best female workers, and the women who remain on the job may not perform at the level at which they are capable.

It is important to remember that affirmative action is one among many social policies that are needed: by itself, it is not enough. In order to effect a change in workers' attitudes, multiple issues should be addressed, beginning at the level of family and elementary school education. For example, certain types of problems—such as barriers to developing male–female friendships due to prejudices, *machismo*, or insecurity—arise from the system in which we live. Although it will not be easy to change these cultural patterns from one day to another, interventions must be made in the communication processes that transmit social representations of gender.

Recognition that equity is good for everyone is the most interesting line of argument in the experiences under analysis.

Examination of Mexico

A governmental decision to take serious action on workplace discrimination against women means that it is willing to reconfigure its concepts of workplace justice from a gender perspective. Without affirmative action programs, little substantial change will take place or be lasting in the long term. In our cultural context, permeated to date by sexist stereotypes and value assessments based on sex, what is needed is a deliberate plan for achieving parity, so that changes that will inevitably occur due to regionalization and NAFTA happen more quickly and are less costly in terms of human suffering and productivity.

The crucial factor in the design of governmental programs meant to eliminate and lessen the effects of workplace discrimination against women is precisely a new conception of workplace justice that recognizes sexual difference and takes problems stemming from gender into consideration.

In Mexico, there is much to be done, because traditional ideas about gender are still widespread—for example, that women and men should occupy different spheres, and that there are "natural" and exclusively masculine or feminine jobs. The fundamental difference between a policy that prevents discrimination and one that remedies it is that a reactive policy depends on the victim's response, whether in the form of speaking out or taking legal action in order to halt discrimination. The advantage of pushing for change within a governmental structure is that prevention has a significant impact. Several studies have shown evidence of sexist beliefs: that a woman's place is in the home, or that women who work are unfaithful to their husbands. It is important to understand how these prejudices affect the way women's work is valued. There is a preponderance of studies that show that when people see two jobs performed in the same manner, they tend to place less value on the one they think was done by a woman. It has been proven many times that a woman is not judged on her performance or on her individual merits, but in terms of the characteristics ascribed to her by her sex alone.

Thus, plans for social communication become a crucial tool for enacting affirmative action. Culture must be considered in order to create effective and well-designed programs without provoking a negative response; these programs attempt to build women's self-esteem, contributing to the improvement of relations between women and men. Affirmative action's ability to combat the cumulative effects of subtle or unintentional discrimination lie precisely in confronting discriminatory cultural valuations, specifically "symbolic violence."

For antidiscriminatory actions to be effective, a plan of action with a multiplicity of measures to change the different factors that affect women's workplace performance must be implemented. This plan should be formulated from a general vision and a political posture; it requires the creation of a specific coordinating agency, similar to the Women's Bureau, as well as a series of guidelines. But, before antidiscriminatory measures become a legal obligation, some companies should be selected to start pilot programs on a voluntary basis. The preparation of company staff allows for supervising and monitoring program implementation. In addition, pilot programs aid in identifying the cultural factors that will help both to build and to expand a realistic program that is in line with national needs. At the same time, it is essential to put together a progressive discourse that can be broadcast through a campaign in the media.

The future of affirmative action depends on its capacity to withstand political questioning, especially from conservative groups that feel threatened by the challenges that question the system of cultural mandates about what is "proper" for men and "proper" for women. Concretely, these groups will express their concern about the supposed disintegration of the family. These criticisms make it necessary to show that affirmative action policies work to achieve certain objectives without trampling on the rights and interests of men, and that they actually strengthen family unity. In addition, it is crucial to bring together a substantial number of union and women's groups to speak out openly in favor of this initiative.

Last, it must be remembered that, even when affirmative action corrects labor inequalities, this policy cannot fix every problem. The country's general economic policy also has consequences. Equality of opportunities for women and men requires a serious investment in social security and in related services (childcare, afterschool programs). In terms of social security worldwide, there have been a number of legislative modifications, because, due to social change, the dependent caregiver woman is no longer the norm.

European governments argue that the first condition for equality of treatment is the existence of social services. The current trend in social security is toward the development of individual rights. Under this structure, a person has rights to a benefit in their own name, independent of their familial situation or marital status. The tendency is toward decreasing or eliminating derived rights (in which a person has rights to a benefit due to a connection of dependency, supposed or real, that joins this person with the insured individual).

In order to maximize women's participation in the workplace in Mexico, it is essential not only to deal with questions related to sexual difference and gender, but also to face the challenge of building a new culture of work and social security. The difficult process of modernizing production in Mexico gives rise to governmental institutions and legal mechanisms and, above all, to a profound renewal of workplace justice. This process cannot happen without the responsible participation of women, who have much to say about the failings of the backward workplace situation.

CHAPTER 3

Gender: Some Conceptual and Theoretical Clarifications[1]

The concept of *gender* emerged at the end of the 1950s. In the 1960s, its use became more widespread in the psychomedical field. Feminism in the 1970s made it more relevant for other disciplines, and by the 1980s, the term had gained strength academically in the social sciences. *Gender* came into public prominence in the 1990s and, in this new century, has become firmly established as "the" explanation for inequality between the sexes. This move from an analytical category to causal force or *explanans*[2] has to do with the fact that the concept became, in itself, a way of understanding the sociocultural origin of women's subordination. In addition, one must note the broad dissemination in political institutions and multilateral agencies of the "vision" denominated as the *gender perspective.* International agencies such as the World Bank and the Interamerican Bank began to grant loans to governments under the condition that they utilize a *"gender* perspective." Thus, this concept has attained a profound cultural impact beyond its academic meaning, and its use has been politicized. And, since what is at stake in the concept of *gender* is an idea about women's role in society, it provokes a reaction from hard-line conservative groups. The Vatican held fast to its immutable explanation that the social subordination of women is a "natural" consequence of sexual difference and, therefore, God's plan; this led an all-out attack on *gender*.[3] Nevertheless, this term gave rise to the phenomenon that Carlos Monsiváis has called "social contagion," by which feminist discourse filtered down in an understandable way to large sectors of the population and popularized an aspiration for equality between women and men. This is why in Mexico, despite conservative pressure, by 1997 the term *gender* was completely integrated into the political discourse, and even the PAN employed it in their electoral platform "Democracy for a Good Government." It is not surprising, then, that in 2000, in his inaugural speech, President Vicente Fox promised that his government would use a "*gender* perspective."

But in addition, *gender* has become a euphemism that incorporates several things: women, relations between the sexes, and feminism. This ambiguity conceals the fact that there is discrimination or oppression, as in, for example, the use of the cliché "that happens because of *gender*." Saying "an issue of *gender*" sounds less harsh than saying "a problem of sexism." In the same way, in daily, colloquial speech, it is increasingly common to hear, "It's a question of *gender*" when alluding to something having to do with women. In this way, addressing the "advance of *gender*"* refers to the leadership positions assumed by women in the last part of the century, when they occupy more public positions and have a growing political presence. This conflation of *gender* with women is old and is repeated in all fields, even in academia.

---

* Translator's note: In Spanish, the phrase is "*avance de género*."

Interpretative communities are constructed to the extent that they share certain meanings and are linked together in processes. Beyond the triumph of *gender perspective* as a mandatory element of public policies, its real success lies in that the understanding of this perspective implies a conceptual leap: a recognition that masculine and feminine behaviors do not depend in an essentialist manner on biological facts, but rather, that they are largely social constructions. Thus, the idea of *gender perspective* is a return to the central principle of feminist discourse.

At the beginning of the 1990s, as the conservative attack on the use of the term *gender* gained international prominence at UN conferences in Cairo and Beijing, academic thought on *gender* took an interesting turn. The feminist academic community received a strong impetus in its production of theories and thinking about *gender* as a result of the intellectual stir caused by the political tensions present everywhere on the world stage. In anthropology, philosophy, linguistics, history, literary criticism, and psychoanalysis, new theorizations were presented on the subject and on the genesis of identity that interpreted the production of alterity based on relational and imaginative processes and referred to the fusion of subjectivity and culture. Thus, the relationship between the symbolic and the social, the construction of identity and the capacity for conscious action (agency), became privileged objects of study.

Use of the concept in several disciplines led to considerable interdisciplinary and transnational crisis surrounding the real meaning of *gender*.[4] Part of the confusion stemmed from the multidisciplinary perspective and concerned something that Mary Hawkesworth has already documented[5]: as research on *gender* proliferated, so too did the ways in which the term is used by people engaged in theory and research.

I will underscore a few examples of the enormous variety that Hawkesworth has recorded: *gender* was used to analyze the social organization of relationships between women and men; to refer to human differences; to conceptualize the semiotics of the body, sex, and sexuality; to explain the differential distribution of responsibilities and benefits between women and men; to allude to microstrategies of power, and to explain identity and the individual aspirations of women and men. Thus, in the final analysis, *gender* was seen as an individual attribute, an interpersonal relationship, and a means of social organization. *Gender* was also defined in terms of social status, sexual roles, and social stereotypes, as well as with respect to power relations evident in domination and subordination. Similarly, it was observed as a product of attribution, socialization, and disciplinary practices or traditions. *Gender* was described as an effect of language, a question of behavioral conformism, a means of perception, and a structural characteristic of work, power, and cathexis. It was posited in terms of a binary opposition, although it was also noted as a *continuum* of variable and varying factors. Endowed with this wide array of uses and interpretations, *gender* was converted into a kind of epistemological wild card that explained what happens between the sexes in a tautological way: everything was a product of *gender*.

In the limited space of this essay, it would be impossible to trace the multiple trajectories of prolific feminist academic thought, which has added significant nuances and clarifications to the initial conceptualization of *gender*. Therefore, I will focus solely on some of the relevant critiques and contributions that have arisen with the application of this concept in my discipline—anthropology—but which are theoretically useful to the remainder of the social sciences.[6] In the field of anthropology, the concept of *gender* understood as the symbolization made by humans, taking the different sex-uation of their bodies as a reference point, has been in use for more than three decades.[7] The prevalence of a dualistic, symbolic way of thinking, which is inherent in the Western, Judeo-Christian tradition and is implicitly reproduced in the majority of intellectual postures, connects universal sexual asymmetry with a practically static, binary way of thinking, defining what is masculine and what is feminine, linking women to nature and men to culture. It has been an unend-ing task to deconstruct this idea in the subsequent devel-opment of the theory of *gender* relations in anthropology. Many women researchers have revealed the way in which women and men are imagined as being in a dichotomous opposition within different cultural traditions. All of these cultures locate an "essence" that distinguishes one sex from another in biological characteristics.

The invariable traits of biological differences have led cul-tures to conceive the symbolization that we now call *gender* as a semiotic apparatus that adheres to a dual, universal pat-tern, defined by sexuation. Feminist anthropologists have been divided on the subject of the universality of feminine subordination. A prominent group argued, based on field research, that reality contradicted the binary emphasis of human classification schemes.[8] In subsequent development of the theory of *gender* relations in anthropology, the critique of the dichotomous opposition between men and women led to a resistance to understanding the founding character of sexual difference.

Toward the end of the 1980s, a handful of women anthro-pologists involved in "feminist ethnography" demonstrated the hermeneutical weaknesses resulting from a nonreflexive perspective. This critique was part of a much more widespread epistemological positioning with important implications for social research grouped under the umbrella term of poststructuralism. The interesting aspect of the proponents of this line of thought was that they showed through field research that reality contradicted the structuralist emphasis on binary classification schemes. With a wealth of ethnographic material, they embarked upon a distinct line of interpretation that went far beyond recording cultural expressions of the symbolization of gender. I take two essays as paradigmatic examples: one by Sylvia Yanagisako and Jane Collier, and another by Marilyn Strathern.[9]

Yanagisako and Collier, both from the United States, revitalized the debate in the anthropological field by questioning whether sexual difference was really the universal foundation for cultural categories of masculine and feminine. They asserted that differentiating between nature and culture was a Western phenomenon, and that distinctions between reproduction and production, public, and private were part of this way of thinking, and not universal cultural precepts. They argued against the idea that cross-cultural variations of *gender* categories were simply diverse modifications and extensions of the same basic fact. This questioning, which they situated at the heart of kinship theory, was interpreted at first as mere provocation, but it marked the beginning of a healthy, irreverent attitude by criticizing the established premises of the field of the anthropology of *gender*.

Parallel to the work of Yanagisako and Collier and their goal of dismantling the universalist line of thinking, the British anthropologist Marilyn Strathern analyzed how inequalities of *gender* emerged by looking at agency in a specific society: the Hagen people of New Guinea in Melanesia. By describing the arrangements of *gender* and the social conditions that produce these, Strathern showed that, in this society, the significance of the masculine and the feminine could be altered depending on the context. She found that Hagen cultural practices grant women an active role in the construction of social meaning; furthermore, she pointed out that the categories of *gender* did not cover the entire array of possibilities for action and positioning of individual women and men. For this very reason, individuals were not limited by being female or male. This perspective differed completely from the traditional viewpoint, which held that women's and men's behavior was constrained by the ideological model of their society. That is why the nature-culture dichotomy, which supposedly produces inequality between women and men, did not apply in the case of the Hagen. Strathern's key assertion was that the typical meaning of *gender* does not hold across all cultures.

Thus, these anthropologists dismantled the dualistic interpretation by arguing that the distinctions between nature and culture, reproduction and production, or public and private were not universal cultural precepts and by refusing to apply a general cross-cultural meaning for *gender*. In addition, by showing how Western thinking impedes an understanding of a nonbinary symbolization, these researchers showed that the symbolic effectiveness of *gender* is not uniform, but rather inconsistent. With this type of argument, at the end of the 1980s and the beginning of the 1990s, several feminist anthropologists began the task of clarifying the conceptual and theoretical terminology related to the processes of symbolization of sexual difference.[10]

The work of elucidating two basic terms—*gender* and sex—became increasingly important; however, something significant was left aside: the formulation of new questions. Already at the beginning of the 1980s, Michelle Z. Rosaldo had pointed out that the problem faced by feminist anthropologists was not lack of information or ethnographic descriptions of women, but rather, the lack of new questions. Rosaldo called for a pause in order to think critically on the type of inquiry that feminist research posited for anthropology and raised the issue of the paradigm being utilized for interpretative work. She clearly established that the particular interpretative frame limits or constrains thinking: what can come to be known will be determined by the type of questions that we learn to ask.[11]

Which paradigm of *gender* did not lead to the formulation of new questions? Initially, in the 1970s, the *sex/gender* system was referred to as the set of arrangements through which the raw material of sex and human procreation was shaped by social intervention and symbolization.[12] Afterward, in the 1980s, *gender* was defined as a clear set of guidelines of social expectations and beliefs that structured the organization of collective life and that produced inequality in ways that individuals valued and responded to the actions of women and men. This set of guidelines makes both women and men into buttresses for a system of reciprocal rules, prohibitions, and oppressions that were marked and sanctioned by the symbolic order. Men and women contribute equally to the maintenance of this symbolic order, reproducing themselves and the system with roles, tasks, and practices that change depending on time and place. And although in the 1990s it is assumed that human beings are the result of historical and cultural production, it is increasingly unclear what is meant by sexuation. Concluding that the subject does not exist prior to operations of the social structure, but rather, that it is produced by symbolic representations within given social formations, should not ignore the materiality of sexed bodies. It is one thing to distinguish the varied and changing forms of symbolization, and yet another to recognize that if certain practices and desires are persistent, one should at least consider the possibility that instead of everything really being the product of the process of symbolization, sexual difference itself might condition some of these differences. The formulation that women and men are not a reflection of a "natural" reality forces us once again to posit the question of the nature of sexual difference.

The theoretical discussion that emerges out of this point has to do with essentialism: the belief that there is something intrinsically different between women and men. Beyond the stimulating discussions of evolutionists and the success of some popularly disseminated texts,[13] the valuable part of this debate is that it broadens the scope of politics and leads to reflection on the voice of women.

One of the most pressing dilemmas for feminism is that a substantial part of the movement posits the need to do politics precisely "as women." Thus, it is a challenge to construct a mobilizing political discourse that includes an analysis of the body without falling into "essentialisms." When feminism appeals to a universal political subject—women—is it or is it not making an essentialist move? The way to answer this question really depends on the theoretical perspective being used: a substantialist essentialism is not the same as a strategic essentialism, as Gayatri Spivak has suggested.[14]

Previously, a more critical sector of the feminist movement explored the implications of referring to women as a political unit with the same interests and needs. In questioning whether a woman speaks only as an agent or representative of her sex, they reached the conclusion that she also speaks marked by a culture, a social class, an ethnic or racial belonging, by her particular sexuality or religion, in short, by her particular history or social positioning.[15] Nevertheless, it is more common for feminists to refer to women in this way, without making distinctions, as if dealing with a collective subject.

If women and men are not an image of "natural" reality, what is the nature of sexual difference? The idea that the subject does not exist prior to the functioning of the social structure, but rather, that the subject is produced by symbolic representations within given social formations consequently leads to the erasure of the materiality of bodies. However, human beings are not sexless; they are sexed beings. And although varied and changing forms of symbolization exist, a question remains: are these practices solely the product of the process of symbolization, or perhaps some of them are conditioned by certain biological differences?

In addition to the refining of this line of thought as the theory and research progressed, a wave of debates arose in the wake of Judith Butler's formulation of *gender* as *performance*.[16] Butler defined *gender* as the effect of a set of complementary, regulatory practices that seeks to shape human identities into a hegemonic, dualistic model. Human beings use the hegemonic elements and categories of their culture to think about themselves and to construct their own image and their conception of self. Although Butler begins with the idea that *gender* is central to the process of identity acquisition and the structuring of subjectivity, she highlights the performativity of *gender*, that is, its capacity to open up to resignifications and personal interventions.

In *Gender Trouble*, Butler analyzed the social reality conceived of in the "*gender* code" and showed the way that heterosexist normativity functions in the representational order. But, the weak point in her analysis was to be found in that she did not sufficiently recognize the complex way sexual difference is symbolized.[17] Humans symbolize biological asymmetry through psychic structure and language. The anatomical serves as the foundation for the framework of symbolization, but part of the symbolization is structured in the unconscious. In conceiving *gender* as *performance*, what role is left for psychic structuring?

Several women anthropologists criticized Butler, among these the British theorist Henrietta L. Moore. Having written various essays and books about *gender*, Moore questioned Butler's interpretation of the performativity of *gender*, and she laid out what she describes as a voluntaristic attitude in terms of gender.[18] The implication of Butler's thesis is that since gender is made in culture, it can be unmade is that if sex is a cultural construction, it can be deconstructed. By describing the imposition of a hegemonic model of relations structured dualistically, Butler posited the flexibility of sexual orientation and legitimated its varied practices. But it is precisely due to the unconscious that, even if regulatory practices impose the heterosexual model of sexual relationships, homosexuality and other *queer* variations exist. These illustrate the force of unconscious symbolization and the psychic difficulties of accepting the heterosexist, cultural mandate.

The formulation of *gender* as a *performance* found success among many US women theorists and researchers. But, on the other side of the Atlantic, this idea did not have the same effect. Owing to the rich hermeneutical tradition of psychoanalytic theory in Europe, Butler's work did not have the same impact on the European academy as it did on US academia.[19] The main critique of Butler was that, by reducing sexual difference to a construction of performative and discursive practices, she implicitly denied its structuring quality. This theorist was forced to explain her position in more detail, which she did in a second book that was not as successful, entitled *Bodies That Matter* (1993).

Butler's influence was still widespread, as evidenced by the number of studies that took up her performative sense of gender. Butler has further deepened and transformed her initial ideas. In her book, *Undoing Gender* (2004), in which she focused on sexual practices and the processes of identity transformation, Butler draws closer to the conceptualization of Bourdieu's *habitus* and defines *gender* as "an incessant activity performed, in part, without one's knowing and without one's willing."[20]

Without a doubt, debates about the performative nature of gender enrich thinking on the subject. However, within anthropology, the classical tradition of interpreting culture as a system of symbols continues to predominate. Linguistics posits fundamental questions and influences *gender* studies, which begin to explore how metaphors of sexual difference produce a universe of representations and categories. By taking language as a founding element of the cultural matrix, that is, the primary structure of meanings by virtue of which human experiences become intelligible, it is clear that the "feminine" and the "masculine" are previously present in language. And although *gender* is still defined as the symbolization of sexual difference—symbolization that distinguishes what is proper for men (the masculine) from what is proper for women (the feminine)—it is accepted that human beings are born into a society that possesses a preexisting discourse on women and men that makes them occupy particular social spaces. Gradually, the "gender perspective" is understood as the vision that not only distinguishes the sexuation of the subject speaking, but also whether that subject speaks with a feminine or masculine discourse. Thus, the panorama is opened to other complexities. For example, to what gender does a woman with a masculine discourse belong? What place does she occupy in society? A man's place?

Although no one at this point doubts that gender is, by definition, a cultural and historical construction, it is clear that it has become a problematic term, not just because of the difficulty of understanding the complexity to which it alludes, but also due to the unfortunate, generalized fact of its reification. Over time, *gender* has become a sociologism that reifies social relations, which are seen as its producers, since it fails to explain how the terms masculine and feminine are present in language prior to the wide variety of social organization. In addition to the reification that the concept *gender* has suffered, it has also been converted into an academic fetish.[21] More than ever, what is needed is to demystify *gender* and continue working to clarify its meaning.

Alice Schlegel has made one of the most useful contributions in the anthropological field. She has labored to clarify the meaning of *gender* and conducts her analytical work seeing *gender* as a cultural construct that does not influence the real practices of women and men. She distinguishes between the general gender meaning—what women and men are in a general sense—and the specific gender meaning —what defines *gender* in accordance with a particular location in the social structure or within a given field of action. Schlegel finds that the specific gender meaning in a given instance is sometimes removed from the general gender meaning, and that a number of specific meanings contradict the general meaning.[22]

Schlegel argues that it is possible to clear up much of the confusion between the two meanings if the context is taken into consideration. Women and men, as symbolic categories, are not isolated from the other categories that make up the symbolic system of a society: the context of a particular ideology is the total ideology of the culture. But the contexts of specific gender meanings are the specific, concrete situations in which women and men come into contact. The meaning attributed to *gender* has more to do with social reality than with the way that these meanings fit with other symbolic meanings. Thus, contradictions arise in daily practices. Schlegel uses her research with the Hopi people in the United States as an example and indicates how many ethnographies allude to the general meanings that are inferred by rituals, myths, literature, even though the specific meanings are not analyzed. She says that these specific meanings vary considerably because they are intersected by questions of status and hierarchy; the particular attitudes of one sex toward another can also disagree from the general meaning. In the general gender meaning, there is a way in which the behavior of women and men is perceived, evaluated, and expected, but in the specific gender meaning, multiple variations are found in actual behavior. She mentions that all societies have produced great variability of practices, in the specific meaning, and that this at times is in opposition to the general meaning. In addition, the apparent contradictions in the cultural mandates on masculinity and femininity refer to the fact that, while human beings are a species with two sexes,[23] the mixed-sex couples may not be only husband and wife, but also other types, for example, father and daughter, grandmother and grandson, brother and sister, aunt and nephew, etc. These differences introduce hierarchical factors, due to age or kinship, which invert or modify the general meanings of *gender*. Therefore, the first step in an analysis of *gender* should be the definition of the general and the specific meanings, in order to explore how the former arises and how the latter takes on shapes that end up contradicting the general meaning.

For Schlegel, it is clear that the categories through which the *sex/gender* systems come to naturalize, sexual difference are always ideal constructions, and that the concrete lives of individuals, the experiences of their bodies and their identities, go far beyond this dualism. This is very much in line with what Virginia Goldner, a psychoanalyst, asserts: the existence of an epistemological paradox with respect to *gender*.[24] The paradox is that *gender* is a false truth since, on the one hand, the binary masculine-feminine opposition is supraordinate, structural, foundational, and transcends any concrete relationship; thus, masculine-feminine, as reified forms of sexual difference, are a truth. But, this truth is false to the extent that concrete variations of human life exceed any binary framework of *gender*. There is a multitude of cases that do not fit into the dual definition.

By presenting these types of clarifications and nuances, the idea of the *gender* system as primordial, transhistoric, and essentially immutable[25] is eroded, and a new understanding of gender's malleability emerges. This has more to do with social reality than with the way that the formal declarations about the "masculine" and the "feminine" fit with other symbolic meanings. In addition, there is an emerging understanding of what Muriel Dimen, an anthropologist, observed, namely, that *gender* is sometimes something central and sometimes something marginal; sometimes it is something definitive, and at others it is contingent.[26] And so, by making the role of *gender* relative, there are more factors contributing to the repeal of the interpretative line that links, nearly as a cultural axiom, men to domination and women to subordination.

Despite these unquestionable advances, at the end of the 1990s, a question remains. Even though it is accepted that the symbolic order establishes the different assessments of value of the sexes for the speaking subject, is it possible to ascertain what belongs to *gender* and what to sex? The question is present in other inquiries. If sex is also a cultural construction, what makes it different from *gender*? Isn't this giving the same thing another name? How would it be possible to defuse the symbolic power of sexual difference, which produces such confusion and/or instability in the categories of sex and *gender*?

In itself, the problem is difficult, and has been even more so for many feminist anthropologists in view of their misunderstanding of social constructivism. Social constructivism stems from an antiessentialist position, which grants great importance to history and processes of change. But, although social constructivism "need not stand against the material world and the exigencies of biology,"[27] many women anthropologists have avoided getting into the debate on the implications and consequences of sexuation, a debate that persists among evolutionary anthropologists.[28] However, there comes a time when it is no longer possible to ignore the consequences of sexual difference on the human body.

In addition, the issue is very politically charged, since sexual difference in procreation has been used to posit their "natural" complementarity of the sexes. Through the process of symbolization, reproductive complementarity has been extrapolated to the social and political realms. Symbolically, the two bodies have been seen as complementary entities. Thus, taking reproductive interdependence as a starting point, social roles and the emotions of men and women have been defined as also interdependent and complementary.

Thousands of years ago, the first sexual division of work established a difference between masculine and feminine spheres. Nevertheless, subsequent human development has substantially altered the facts of this first division, symbolized in the separation of the private and public sphere. Although the two bodies mutually depend on each other for the species' continuity, they are not necessarily complementary in other areas. Interpreting reproductive complementarity as conclusive evidence of an absolute complementarity is misguided and fraught with perils. This type of thinking lead to the idea that women's domain should be the private sphere and men's the public, which has led to well-known forms of exclusion and discrimination against women. But anatomical differences are not expressions of deeper differences; they are just that, biological differences. In order to achieve clarity, it is essential to historicize the process of the sexual division of work and deconstruct the social resignifications of procreation.

The impact of pregnancy and birth on human life is expressed in a multiplicity of ways. One of these expressions, the ontological perplexity surrounding procreative difference, has given rise to a mystification of heterosexuality: rampant heterosexism. This deception is the ideological basis for homophobia. Reproduction must be separated from sexuality. The belief that human sexuality requires complementarity is a serious error of interpretation. The reproductive function of women and men does not determine erotic desires or feelings of love. In addition to this point, anthropological reflection confronted the persistent tendency to give biology more weight than other disciplines in explanations of questions of human nature.

Without question, the current rift between the social and biological disciplines makes it difficult to clearly identity the implications that sexuated anatomy has had on human beings in the production of certain cultural processes.[29] Sexuation has played an essential role in the social conditions of the production of culture; this role has undergone changes throughout history, just as the process of human procreation has been transformed. Recently, the worldwide development of new reproductive technologies has created a vital need for in-depth thinking on the relationship between biology and culture. These unprecedented forms of procreation—a paradigmatic example of the human capacity to exceed the limitations of biology and impose culture—have shaken the established assumptions of Western ideology regarding kinship.[30]

Thus, at the end of the twentieth century and the beginning of the twenty-first, biology returns to importance in feminist thinking on social relations. The complex relationship between biology and culture demands not only rigorous analyses of the importance of sexuation in the practices of women and men, but also the understanding that social and political inequality between the sexes is a product of human relations. This inequality has less to do with the resources and capacities of individuals than with the beliefs that guide the way people act and construct their comprehension of the world. But is it possible to link certain aspects of social inequality with sexual asymmetry? As there are patterns that repeat themselves, one must not solely concentrate on specific, local forms of social relations, but rather, one must dare to explore the realm of biology. Paradoxically, despite theoretical advances, there are still barriers to recognition that the place of women and men in human social life is not only a product of the meaning that their activities acquire through concrete social interactions, but also of what humans are on a biological level. For this reason, although in human social life, biology is more an excuse for than a cause of inequality, it is increasingly crucial to investigate the interaction with the biological. This is why it is imperative to build bridges between the social and natural sciences.[31]

In terms of recognizing links to biology, the work of Henrietta Moore stands out. In 1999, she published a critical essay entitled "Whatever Happened to Women and Men? Gender and Other Crises in Anthropology." Moore looks at the theoretical limitations of anthropological discourse on the topics of *gender*, sex, and sexuality, and conducts a cross-cultural comparison of the history of anthropological thought in relation to the varied conceptualizations of the individual and the self. Her treatment of the subject draws on poststructural theories and psychoanalysis. She also notes a change in the conceptualization of gender: "Where formerly gender had been conceived as the cultural elaboration of a sex that preceded it, now gender became the discursive origin of sex."[32] Based on her understanding of psychoanalysis, Moore takes issue with attempts to reduce sexual difference to a construct of historically contingent discursive practices. She also questions the rejection of the idea that there is something invariable in sexual difference. In this way, she reviews the terms of the *sex-gender* debate that arose in relation to the classic inquiry about whether nature or culture is the determining factor. This inquiry takes different forms: essentialism versus constructivism, or substance versus signification. Moore reminds her readers that Freud was one of the first to point out the limitations of this kind of formulation by positing that neither anatomy nor social conventions could explain the existence of sex by themselves. She also argues that Lacan went one step further when he said that sexuation is not a biological phenomenon, because one must use language and representation in order to take on a sexuated position: sexual difference is produced in the realm of the symbolic.[33]

Moore states that, even if it is apparent that sex and *gender* are not the same, there is no need to draw a rigid boundary between the two, since the borders are in motion: human beings are able to vary their practices, to play with their identities, to resist hegemonic cultural impositions. Nonetheless, one must not confuse the instability of sex and *gender* categories with the disappearance or blurring of men and women as we know them physically, symbolically, and socially. Moore indicates that the sexuation of bodies will not be able to be understood if one thinks of sex as a social construction. Her intellectual dilemma deals with the possibility of reconciling theories based on the unconscious with those based on willful decision-making, static structures of linguistic difference with the performative and the discursive, the register of the symbolic with that of the social. Thus, she posits the need to develop an interpretive perspective that recognizes the complex relationship between materialism and social constructivism.[34]

As feminist anthropologists attempting to work with the concept of *gender*, we must return to Moore's approach and, in addition to the work of reconciling theories and recognizing complex relationships, acknowledge a point made by Rosaldo twenty-five years ago[35]: what is important is to ask good questions. What would these good questions be today? I do not pretend to known them all, but I do have a fundamental one: if *sexual difference* is not only a social construction, if it is what we could call sex/substance and, at the same time, sex/signification, is there or is there not a contingent relationship between the male body and masculinity and the female body and femininity? Solving this mystery is indispensable if we are to clarify the social consequences of the biological dissymmetry between the males and the females of the species. Are the masculine and the feminine arbitrary transcriptions in a neutral or indifferent consciousness? There is no doubt that the fact that the female body or the male body has a previous social value has an effect on the consciousness of women and men. But, although the weight of history and culture is recognized, to what extent does a large part of the signification of *gender* have its roots in biology? These lines of inquiry lead us back to a question with a political tinge: if both femininity and masculinity (in the sense of *gender*) are more than mere socialization and conditioning, if they are something more than a discursive category without a material referent, that is, if they have something to do with biology, will it be possible to eliminate the social inequality between the sexes? This political dilemma is echoed in the theory: how to accept sexual difference as something foundational without it ending up outside history and resistant to change?

Individuals occupy differentiated positions in the cultural and political order, because they are marked by their sexuation and by a series of factors, ranging from economic, cultural, and political circumstances to the particular development of their psychic life. Deciphering their situational and relational positioning as human beings demands not only more research, but also a better theorization of the complex intersection between the cultural, biological, and psychic. This theorization requires concepts that span both dimensions. *Habitus*[36] is one such concept, which means simultaneously a product (the cultural fabric) and a generating principle of practices and regulations. With *habitus*, it is understood that human practices are not only reproductive strategies determined by the social conditions of production, but also are themselves produced by subjectivities. Another relevant concept is that of embodiment,[37] which communicates the idea of the concrete presence of the body and its sensorial subjectivity. The process of embodiment of cultural prescriptions in the body is more determining than the corporality of difference in terms of the anatomical difference between women and men. The concepts of *embodiment* and *habitus* turn out to be very useful in the analysis of *gender* systems, that is, in the ways that societies organize the cultural classification of human beings.

One cannot conceive people solely as social constructions or anatomical units.[38] Both of these reductionist visions are ineffective at uncovering the articulation of what is at play in each dimension: flesh (hormones, biochemical processes); mind (culture, social prescriptions, traditions), and unconscious (desires, drives, identifications). The body is more than the subject's "container." The body is mind, flesh, and unconscious, and it is symbolized in two areas: the psychic and the social. The unconscious representation of the body necessarily passes through imaginary and symbolic representation. However, although the body is the juncture point of the psychic and the social, essentializing its dual biological nature can lead us to make unsettling simplifications, for example, believing that because of sexuation men and women have different thought processes. Thus, the challenge is twofold: recognizing sexual difference, while at the same time stripping it of its determinist connotations.

Among the most required issues in the field of anthropology is to take a critical approach to sexuation, while at the same time valuing its centrality for psychic life. Those who are interested in research and reflection on *gender* should take heed of the intersection of sexual difference and the psychic dimension, and the resultant processes of identification it provokes. *Gender* relations are the most intimate of social relations in which we are implicated, and much of the construction of *gender* takes place in the realm of subjectivity. One must constantly remember that the development of our relational processes includes an unconscious part of our beliefs on sexual difference.

Although for a long time psychoanalysis defined the self as a relational construct, this is also now understood as an effect of the social construction of *gender*. That is, the symbolization of sexual difference is a process that structures subjectivities. In this respect, one of the great challenges for anthropology today is analyzing the cultural construction of subjectivities. Moore points out that, in a certain way, this is "the continuation of old debates about the relationship between structure and agency."[39] This is of utmost importance for the increased awareness that frequently comes about during fieldwork. This change in consciousness increases the capacity for action of the subjects that we study and with whom we spend time and relate. For this reason, anthropology should broaden its thinking to explore the impact of *gender* in a number of identificatory processes.

For all of the aforementioned reasons, I insist on the need to have a real *gender* perspective in the anthropological field, even though the improper uses and ambiguous meanings of the concept of *gender* have not yet been eliminated. Some, fed up with the confusion concerning definitions, have renounced the use of this category and spurn this interpretative perspective. Joan W. Scott, a US historian, author of one of the most important essays on *gender*,[40] made a useful point in a later work: one should read the confusion, discord, and identification still being made between sex and *gender* as *symptoms* of certain recurring problems.[41] Perhaps we could take a problem denounced by Bourdieu as an example of this type of *symptom*: "the *relative dehistoricization* and *eternalization* of the structure of the sexual division and the corresponding principles of division."[42] Bourdieu proposes detecting the "*historical* mechanisms responsible" for these perverse processes, in order "to reinsert into history, and therefore to restore to historical action, the relationship between the sexes that the naturalistic and essentialist vision denies them."[43]

Finally, I have reached the conclusion that if one seeks to explore or reflect on *gender*, it is necessary to refine one's analysis with its inherent complexity always in mind. Among other things, this entails keeping in mind the three dimensions of the body. Many errors in the conceptual use of gender have to do with avoiding references to sexuation. One should not avoid the biological aspect; likewise, one should not privilege it, repeating explanations that have a sole focus on biological processes. Although there are no clear formulations at present that would allow for better understanding of our complex object of study, it is important to be open to the complexity of theoretical and conceptual issues. This is why I think it is appropriate to remember what a Spanish writer, José María Guelbenzu, pointed out in regard to clarity and complexity.[44] In reference to literature, he said that the more the elements of a story are outlined and examined, the more complex the narration becomes and, paradoxically, the clearer the situations. Complexity and clarity are not conflicting terms. As the reader follows the drama of the characters, complexity is what allows her to have clarity when reaching conclusions about them.

By simply accepting the complexity of the symbolization of sexual difference, there could be enough clarity to analyze the multiple dimensions of the relations between the sexes. Theory is necessary not only to facilitate the indispensable change in paradigms about the human condition, but also to stop discriminatory practices that translate difference into inequality. Observing how the reductionist havoc of the dualistic interpretation of *gender* reverberates in feminist political proposals, the urgency of clarifying these questions is apparent. If increasing capacity for conscious action (agency) is a goal of feminism, one of the responsibilities of feminist anthropologists who are politically committed to this cause is to develop the reflective tools that mobilize the potential consciousness of their political base. The fruits of knowledge also feed collective action. This is precisely why theory is not a luxury, but a necessity.

CHAPTER 4

Feminisms: Disagreements and Arguments[1]

To Lucero Gónzalez, who taught me the value of friendship
when facing disagreements.

The Function of Arrogance

"When do debate and discussion become a fight, a *querelle* and when does a *disputatio* become a dispute? At what point do argument and argumentation become entrenched antagonisms?"[2] These questions posed by Beatrice Hanssen condense a set of problems present in Latin American feminisms. This is why, when Gloria Careaga invited me to reflect on the challenges and perspectives of our movement, I thought about exploring the antagonism between self-declared autonomous feminists and those considered "institutionalized." However, I did not want to expound on the usual problems brought about by the nearly religious political lifestyle with its messianic positions, schisms, and priestesses, nor on the typical problems brought about by rivalries between women with their narcissistic attention to the tiniest of differences. In this chapter, I would like to discuss two challenges that imply shortcomings of different orders of magnitude: the first, surmountable with a bit of self-critical awareness, while the other demands more substantial effort. In my opinion, these are the inescapable challenges we have to face.

What is happening in the Latin American movement that prevents us from being able to debate with one another? Understanding that there are other issues at play, I think that what Carlos Pereda has called "arrogant reason" plays a crucial role.[3] This form of dialogue is a shortcoming that can be rectified through self-criticism. In his brief but invaluable essay, Pereda dissects arrogance as a characteristic of identity constructed on certain cultural structures and on a model that affirms itself while discriminating against anything that it does not know or understand. Pereda finds that a good part of the conflict of arrogance arises out of the difficulty of recognizing the other, describing it as a strategy shared by two (un)cultures: the academic and the antiacademic.

Pereda sees arrogance as a means of dividing and being divided in order to defend hierarchies considered unassailable. As an expression of inflexible thinking, as a lack of concern for the opinion of others, arrogance leads to prejudice.

> Thus, arrogance is one of the most effective mechanisms for immunizing oneself against the real or possible interpellations of the other. An arrogant woman or man considers her or himself much too far above those who question her or him to pause and enter into a discussion, to make explanations, to offer arguments.[4]

The result is obvious: "As a consequence, only allies are admitted."[5] For this reason, arrogant reasoning is a form of sectarianism. Sects, understood as groups that hinder both internal and external progress, have what Pereda calls their "theoretical armor." This author posits that the rule of sectarianism is: *More of the same is always good.*[6] In opposition to this saying is what is, by definition, the antisectarian rule:

> Don't forget that any kind of inclination has a limit, a ceiling: beyond it there is madness and emptiness. In both cases, little by little or all of a sudden, the absurdity begins.[7]

The message is clear: persisting blindly with any idea or "inclination,"* without opening oneself to any others leads to a lack of productiveness and exhaustion.

In order to be productive participants in a dialogue instead of sterile adversaries in the ever more urgent debate about Latin American feminism, we must work together to dismantle this arrogant reasoning, both in intellectual and antiintellectual spaces. There is no need to do anything loud or blatant or spectacular: just an exercise of reason without fear of changing one's mind or admitting mistakes. In order to achieve this, one must listen, attempt to understand the reasons and lack of reasons of other feminists, study, and learn to debate and make arguments. But, what is needed for these new discursive strategies, founded on the elimination of antipathy and sectarianism, to be effective? To question one another, to dialogue, to confront ideas and arguments. To do this, one of the essential elements is to build a base level of understanding, which entails minimizing the terminological confusion and sharing certain codes. This is the second challenge, which demands another kind of effort.

While we as feminists easily locate the source of our problems in the outside world, the "patriarchy," other feminists,

---

* Translator's note: In Spanish, the term used is *querencia*.

differences, we have a difficult time naming and politically articulating issues that are in the air. This capacity for perceiving what is around us increases when there is a theoretical perspective. Although the diversification and proliferation of positions makes it imperative to speak of multiple feminisms, it is striking to note the repeated mention of a shared desire to sustain an open political debate. Nevertheless, among the silent assumptions that circulate among us is the one that holds that broad debate demands plain, direct language and obliges us to avoid difficult terminology.

At the risk of being labeled an elitist, I believe it is essential to distinguish among different spheres of debate with their own specific requirements. To achieve a certain level of political discussion, one must recognize the cognitive differences between our varied contexts and attempt to understand each other at a theoretical base level that might allow for the exchange of ideas. Achieving this is not easy, since in addition to subjective resistance, there is a prejudice that spending time on theoretical questions takes time away from praxis. I believe precisely the opposite: certain theoretical notions improve praxis. Judith Butler coined the term *theoretical activism* to recognize the value of theoretical reflection, in the face of those who posit theory as a complicated universalism and defend pragmatism as the correct political practice.[8]

In contemporary Latin America, theory needs to be updated, not only due to an urgent process of political *aggiornamento*, but also due to lack of growth in the movement.[9] What has caused young women's rejection of and/or indifference to feminism? Among other things, it has to do with our repetitive and boring discourse, due to the lack of new theoretical formulations. In addition, a considerable number of feminists from different Latin American countries have remained stuck in the fetishized fad of *gender*.[10] This could be a result of what Bourdieu and Wacquant[11] have called "the ruses of imperialist reason," which operate, for example, by means of the imposition of research agendas promulgated by US *doxa* through its universities and foundations; however, this could also be due to our own limitations: self-censuring of thinking is more powerful than any external prescription. The consequence of the fetishized use of the *gender* paradigm is a simplification of human conflicts, which does not incorporate the complex dimensions of the body and which feeds a naïve political voluntarism. Bourdieu and Wacquant assert that some "isolated terms, which appear technical," are more insidious than theories or philosophical visions of the world, since they condense and circulate "an entire philosophy of the individual and social organization." In order to avoid this danger, one must move away from the comfortable path laid out by certain ideological certainties—in which the concept of *gender* occupies a politically correct position—and set off on a more risky path regarding differences between men and women.

The Place of Theory

How do we present our ideas when we enter into debate? Do we make explicit the theoretical apparatus that we are using? Do we make the paradigm at the base of our work clear? Clarity leads to more dialogue and less confrontation. Although theory per se is valuable, it becomes a tool for those of us in a political movement to mold ourselves into participants, rather than adversaries, in a conversation.

What are we feminists referring to when we speak about "theory?" "Feminist theory" has gone from being a political and ideological discourse to occupying a prominent position in universities and research centers in developed nations. A quick review of the theoretical production shows intense activity, from literary criticism to political philosophy, from *queer theory* to psychoanalytic theory, from cultural criticism to anthropology. But when "feminist theory" is mentioned, it principally alludes to a change in cognitive paradigms that propose a new reading of the human condition. Feminist theory has undertaken both a deciphering of the situational and relational determinism of human beings, as well as a series of theorizations regarding the discriminatory consequences of the symbolization of sexual difference.

Roiling around sexual difference is one of the most pressing feminist debates: the battle over essentialism. For feminists, dealing with this subject becomes unavoidable, not only because we have much more invested emotionally and politically in the subject of "woman" than we realize, but also because a substantial sector of the movement posits the need to engage in politics, precisely "as women." For this reason, our challenges have to do with how to analyze the body without slipping into essentialisms and with how to construct a mobilizing political discourse that recognizes sexual difference and gender.

When feminism appeals to a universal political subject (women), is it making an essentialist move? The responses— both affirmative and negative—depend on one's theoretical focus: substantialist essentialism is not the same as strategic essentialism, as Gayatri Chakravorty Spivak has suggested.

Throughout her work, Spivak has dealt with central issues of essentialism, saying different things at different times. A compelling insight that caused a great deal of confusion was her allusion to "strategic essentialism." The actual quote, "the strategic use of positivist essentialism in a scrupulously visible political interest,"[12] was interpreted in the following way: in order to politically mobilize a group of women, it is acceptable for us to call for them to engage in politics "as women." Faced with this assertion, the debate ensued: how are strategic essentialism and substantialist essentialism different? Spivak's response was twofold: on the one hand, in order for it really to be strategic, the use of the word "woman" must be accompanied by a persistent critique; if there is not constant critique, then the strategy is frozen in an essentialist position. On the other hand, it depends on who is using the word "woman." It is not the same thing for an intellectual woman to say "I, as a woman" as it is for a working-class woman. What determines whether or not an analysis or statement is strategic or substantialist essentialism? It is the difference between a woman who dares to say "I, as a woman" as her consciousness awakens to the imbalances of social power, and a feminist politician after years of reading and discussions doing the same. The issue that must be clarified is the location of the people who are speaking and the purpose for which they are employing the concept. The who and the how define the what. Here, we can clearly understand Spivak's distinction between essentialism as a strategy (as a situational tool) and essentialism as a theory.[13] However, admitting a need for a strategic premise (such as, "all of us are oppressed as women") to ground our work in order to facilitate processes of openness and communication is not the same as *believing* in a shared essence and defending it.

In politics, a small degree of idealization is necessary to move subjectivities and achieve changes, thus the strategic use of promoting a political awakening. That is why calls for increased personal consciousness are frequently dressed up in essentialist garb, such as the phrase, "You, as a woman." But after this first moment, the movement should do subsequent theoretical work, and each sector must develop its own position regarding the challenge of affirming the importance of sexual difference without essentializing it. Does a woman speak solely as an agent or representative of her sex? No, she also speaks marked by a culture, a social class, an ethnic or racial identification, a certain sexuality, a religion, in fact, a specific history or position. So then, what does it mean to speak of women as a political unit with the same needs and interests?

In her brilliant analysis of the ways women legitimate their public language, Catherine Gallagher reminds us that what brought women out into the streets, what pushed them into the different protests in the feminist struggle, from the suffragist hunger strikes to stand-offs with the police, was "their feeling of loyalty to a community of sisters in suffering: in other words, solidarity with a collective subject."[14] Unarguably, the rhetorical power of the term "woman" has to do with this collective subject. But its acritical use carries with it a risk for political action, for example, by giving rise to the idea that only a woman can really know what happens to another woman: this is a flawed premise, not because it is "essentialist," but because it posits the possibility of knowledge in identity.[15] This is why one is even obliged to monitor language: it is not the same thing to speak "as a woman" as it is to speak "from a woman's body." This subtle distinction, full of meaning, is crucial for our approach to politics.

Intellectual work is indispensable precisely in order to make these subtle distinctions. Theory is not a luxury; it is a vital need. How can we remake the world and power relations between the sexes? Can we take sexual difference as an "ontological" affirmation, as if there were an absolute truth about woman in opposition to that of men?[16] Taking the sexual duality of the subject for granted without any kind of nuances can cause us to slip into unsettling errors, such as affirming that male and female thinking is different because it is sexuated. The challenge is, then, twofold: recognizing sexual difference, while at the same time stripping it of its determinist connotations. This requires accepting that masculine and feminine social behaviors do not essentially depend on the biological facts, and recognizing the specific weight of the complex structure of the human species: the body as flesh, mind, and unconscious.[17]

The differences between the interests and behaviors of men and women are not the consequence of an essence rooted in biology, nor are they solely the result of roles imposed by society. Sexual difference and the context[18] of life experience constitute the subject within her or himself. Individuals occupy differential positions in the cultural and political order, because they are marked by their sexuation and by a series of elements, from economic, cultural, and political circumstances to a particular development of subjectivity.[19] From this theoretical conception arise questions for political action. One crucial issue has to do with civic participation.

It is clear that women and men occupy different positions in society and that this makes it more difficult for women to exercise their rights. However, can sexual difference constitute a principle upon which radically different forms of citizenship are established for the two sexes? How can we defend an egalitarian citizenship and vindicate sexual difference? In the antiintellectual climate we live in, the key role of theory in the development of concepts that are useful for guiding practice is not understood. One example is the inability—or perhaps we should say resistance—to understand sexual difference, in the sense of taking into account its biological substratum and discerning that there is an additional psychic reality at play. This resistance has led to thinking that the differences between masculinity and femininity are only the result of social factors. And although this has begun to receive criticism from a clear-thinking sector of feminists, the reductionist repercussions of this limitation continue to reverberate in the movement's political proposals.

From Discord to Debate

If we see ourselves as participants in a debate around the challenges and perspectives of feminism, what moves us to seek each other out today? The hope for dialogue? The longing for a productive debate? Without a doubt, the possibility for debate is very attractive. But, whether we like it or not, we cannot debate rigorously only among ourselves, without at the same time taking into consideration those who are doing theory in the social sciences, in political philosophy, and in poststructuralist circles.

Feminist theory is intrinsically multidisciplinary: a wide variety of people participate in the debate. Today, feminist theory is addressed not only internally, that is within feminist or gender studies, but also in the wider field of cultural and social criticism. The difficulty that some feminists face in situating themselves in the vast terrain of the theoretical debate seems to derive from a fear that feminism will be subsumed, made secondary, compromised by patriarchal thinking. However, in addition, locating oneself within the broad intellectual context necessitates the appropriation of the rules for theoretical criticism of a specific discipline, that is, a knowledge of the authors and the internal debates, which entails an effort to educate oneself that not all feminists are able or willing to undertake.

Notwithstanding this, our movement must develop a twofold, Janus-faced vision, acknowledging both the internal and external debate. Thus, the movement must invest in what Teresa de Lauretis has formulated as a relational vision to link the intrinsic with the extrinsic.[20] Unfortunately, our internal situation is actually quite sad, because emergent feminist criticism has been unable to arouse the interest of the different cultural and academic establishments. In our region, gender studies do not constitute an important trend within the field of social sciences, nor does feminist thinking have a place in the Latin American intellectual world.

What is going on in the theoretical debate in our countries? Without a doubt, there are cutting-edge academic feminists in Latin America who insert themselves into wider debates in their own fields, but who have not developed much interest in theory. There is no question that feminist research and reflection have allowed for more comprehensive mapping of women's situations in our countries.[21] Despite the deep antiintellectual prejudice in feminist groups, these have provided consistency and visibility to the university programs insofar as they demand research that provides data upon which to base political demands (domestic violence, wage discrimination, abortion, etc.). However, there is a lack of theoretical vitality in the different centers of academic studies on women and gender. This reflects a broader sociocultural phenomenon: in our region, urgent political needs have relegated theoretical discussion to a secondary status. If this occurs within academia, what can we expect from activist groups?

Those who reject theory typically adopt pragmatic attitudes. Influenced by a brutal neopragmatism and irritated by theory's difficult terminology, many feminists find themselves at an impasse—forced to choose one or the other extreme: theory or practice. Other feminists, myself included, believe that both tough pragmatism and an unequivocal defense of pure theory are insufficient for politics, and we continue to argue for the value of linking theory and practice. Nevertheless, if anything is obviously lacking in our movement, it is the use of theory to inform our engagement in politics.

Thus, if we enter into the field of debate with no theoretical apparatus, it would not be surprising for personalized arguments to predominate. Although controversies among First World feminists are sparked by what could be defined as theoretical issues, for us it is not easy to analyze the connections between conflicting positions and theoretical questions. This is why, unlike in other feminisms, the confrontations apparent in the Latin American movement are more indicative of rivalries and personal resentments than of substantive theoretical differences.

This characteristic is associated with another facet of the way that we engage in politics. Many of the arbitrary expressions that circulate in the movement are not only product of "arrogant reason," but also of a kind of blindness to our own limitations. It is already known that feminism gives rise to a "logic of female sameness,"[22] which feeds the feeling that all of us as women are identical[23] and produces a strange dynamic in our exchanges. It has always intrigued me why, despite the fact that we know that rigor is a condition for the serious political debate we long for, we attempt to initiate it without previous preparation, without documents to discuss, without a shared foundation. Thus, sharing the slightest responsibility for holding this debate means two things as well: recognizing our own limitations, and trying to broaden the cognitive and conceptual margins within which we move.

We need the will, discipline, and, above all, enlightenment: *light* and more *light.*

As I am convinced that knowledge, and specifically theory, are vital to deal more effectively with conflicting positions and the construction of alliances and coalitions, I want to end with an example indicative of this hope. Among the various kinds of feminism, there are several basic conceptual and methodological disagreements over fundamental principles and premises. But there is also a certain kind of disagreement about which there has been no theorization within our movement. It is the one that Jacques Rancière locates in a specific situation of speech: "one in which one of the interlocutors at once understands and not understand what the other is saying. Disagreement is not the conflict between one who says white and another who says black. It is the conflict between one who says white and another who also says white but does not understand the same thing by it."[24]

The disagreement is neither a lack of knowledge, nor misunderstanding. The disagreement does not refer to the words: it refers to the actual situation of those speaking, to the production of meanings and significations. The disagreement has less to do with argumentation than with the presence or absence of an object shared by both people. The extreme situation of disagreement is that in which one person does not see the object they share when another person presents it to them. At its base, this extreme situation has to do with politics. What can a person who uses words to debate do, since even though she lends the words her own meanings and inflections, she still assumes that the other person will understand her? Among us, as feminists, a false perception exists that political discord means controversy, and not this kind of disagreement.

It should not surprise us that if we are unable to theorize the nature of the disputes among us, we internalize conflicts that we conceive of in the wrong way. We have to stop thinking that theory is, in itself, patriarchal, elitist, totalizing, and masculinist, or universalist, hegemonic, Western, and imperialist, and attempt to apply it rigorously in our praxis, our experiences, our narratives, our politics of the body.

The terrain of the political is an intersubjective field that is structured both by the rules of public debate (practically nonexistent in Latin America) and by agonistic tensions.[25] Agonism refers not to the confrontation—antagonism—but rather, to the tension inherent in the multiple differences present in the structure of the speaking subject. Therefore, waiting for consensus or agreement would be an error that is not only linked with our subjectivity, but also with our theoretical positioning. A goal for our movement, above all when we are aware of the size and strength of our common enemy, could be to arrive at areas of agreement, progressing in specific coalitions without attempting to erase our differences. This entails not only building another political logic, but also creating new discursive and argumentative practices. The possibility of reaching some moments of alliance is closely linked with the possibility of accommodating our different positions.[26] We have to "compete" and convince. This is why we must force ourselves to develop a theoretical basis for our positions.

Despite facing grave challenges, we, as Latin American feminists, must fling ourselves into the work of articulating "the possibilities of a more fully democratic and participatory political life."[27] One of our tasks is to define points of reference on the lines of intersection. We need to find these points in order to construct a broader alliance and to see ourselves more as participants in a conversation than as adversaries. However, aside from all the work that this challenge demands, there is something urgent that each of us can do starting today by ourselves, with no need for anyone else and with nothing more than a different kind of will: rid ourselves of the "arrogant reason" that for far too many years has prolonged the long night[28] of Latin American feminism.

Notes

Theory in the World: A General Introduction

1. Martin Heidegger, *What Is Called Thinking?*, trans. Fred D. Wieck and J. Glenn Gray. New York: Harper and Row, 1968, p. 166–167.
2. Jacques Derrida, *The Other Heading*, trans. Pascale-Anne Brault and Michael B. Naas (Bloomington: Indiana University Press, 1992).
3. Vincent B. Leitch, ed., *The Norton anthology of theory and criticism* (New York: Norton, 2010).
4. Cited in Henry Louis Gates, Jr., "The Black Letters on the Sign: W. E. B. Du Bois and the Canon," in *The Oxford W. E. B. Du Bois* (New York: Oxford University Press, 2007), vol. 8, p. xvi.
5. Michael Ryan and Julie Rivkin, *Literary Theory: An Anthology* (Malden: Wiley Blackwell, 2004).
6. An example that has stayed with me over the years remains Diane Bell's excellent *daughters of the dreaming* (Minneapolis: University of Minnesota Press, 1993), which, in response to requests for inclusion of third-world material, put in Trin-ti Min-Ha and me, longtime faculty persons in prestigious U.S. universities!
7. My most recent experience is to encounter a Maori activist book-seller and an Indian feminist at such a convention, who had never heard of Frederick Douglass, where only in response to my questions did the South African participant admit to political problems with translation between indigenous languages, and the mainland Chinese participant to the barrier between Mandarin and Cantonese. Examples can be multiplied.

8. I have discussed this in "Inscription: Of Truth to Size," in *Outside in the Teaching Machine* (New York: Routledge, 2009), pp. 201–216

9. See Hermann Herlinghaus, Monika Walter, eds., *Posmodernidad en la periferia: enfoques latinoamericanos de la nueva teoría cultural* (Berlin: Langer, 1994).

1 From Protests to Proposals: Scenes from a Feminist Process

1. *Mujerismo* is a concept that essentializes the state of being a woman, idealizes the "natural" conditions of women, and romanticizes relationships between women. An attitude typical of *mujerismo* is that of speaking in the name of women, as if they all shared the same position in society.

2. Cano 2006.

3. Lau 1987; González 2001; Bartra 2002.

4. Monsiváis 1998.

5. Mouffe 1996.

6. Castellanos 1995.

7. Despite all this, several international delegates make it to the Teatro Eleuterio Méndez in Coyoacán, among them Germaine Greer and Domitila de Chungara.

8. Hirschman 1986.

9. Gelb 1992.

10. Unlike the financing provided in other Latin American countries, as in the cases of the Flora Tristán group in Peru and La Morada in Chile.

11. One publication of this tendency of "popular" feminism, nicknamed *"populárica,"* is *Feminismo y sectores populares en América Latina, Jornadas Feministas,* EMAS, CIDHAL, GEM, MAS, CEM, COVAC, APIS, 1987.

12. A number of feminist groups brought up the need to establish contact with other groups emerging in different parts of the country; they organized the *Encuentros Nacionales* (National Conferences) (1981, 1982, 1983, 1984, and 1989). In addition to these meetings of feminists, there were ten national and sectorial conferences of women workers, *campesinas* (female

agricultural workers), and *colonas* (women involved in the national squatters and land rights movement) between 1980 and the beginning of 1987. On average, there were 500 women in attendance at each conference and at least fifty local or regional meetings of popular feminist groups.

13. Tuñón 1997.
14. Lamas 1986; Mercado 1990.
15. Tarrés 2006.
16. "From Love to Necessity" by Haydée Birgin (Argentina), Celeste Cambría (Peru), Fresia Carrasco (Peru), Viviana Erazo (Chile), Marta Lamas (Mexico), Margarita Pisano (Chile), Adriana SantaCruz (Chile), Estela Suárez (Mexico), Virginia Vargas (Peru), and Victoria Villanueva (Peru). Three feminists—Viviana Erazo, Marta Lamas, and Estela Suárez— were responsible for drafting the essay. It was published in the magazine *Fem*, Year 11, No. 60, December 1987.
17. (1) We feminists are not interested in power; (2) We feminists engage in politics in a different way; (3) We feminists are all equal; (4) There is a natural unity that comes from the sole fact of being women; (5) Feminism only exists as a politics of women with women; (6) The small group is the movement; (7) By their very existence, women's spaces guarantee a positive process; (8) Because, as a woman, I feel something, it's right; (9) The personal is automatically political, and (10) Consensus is democracy.
18. Barcellona 1996: 151–155.
19. Bondi 1996.
20. There is a debate about the translation of this term into Spanish. Some people use *apoderamiento* (see Martha Elena Venier, 1997); others use the neologism "*empoderamiento.*" I prefer the term *potenciación*.
21. The expression emerged during the Sixth Feminist Conference (*IV Encuentro Feminista*) in El Salvador in 1993.
22. These postures are reflected in essays by Francesca Gargallo (1997) and Haydée Birgin (1997).
23. Bondi 1996.
24. Unlike traditional corporativism, which organized collectivity on the foundation of associations representing professional

interests and activities, neocorporativism is structured on certain identities: women; the Indigenous; homosexual. See Mouffe 1996.

25. As a result of the 1988 post-electoral conflicts, the debate about respect for the exercise of citizenship attains visibility. Some sectors develop an analysis of their diverse experiences of civic defenselessness before state power and its various expressions: police; legal; bureaucratic; military, and fiscal. The illegalization of abortion is another experience of the arbitrary nature of the state, except that the radicalized discourse of Mexican feminism does not clearly formulate it in this way, and does not formulate it in such a way that it could be placed on the political agenda of the parties and on the public agenda of the government.

26. The PRD was the first party to grant a quota of 30%. See García, Martínez, and Fernández 1991. Afterward, the PRI followed, see Chapa 1996. The PAN has to date refused to implement quotas.

27. The Information Group on Reproductive Choice (*El Grupo de Información en Reproducción Elegida*, GIRE) is formed in 1991, after the reform to Article 130 of the Constitution in which the Salinas government confers legal status on the Catholic Church. GIRE is founded as a nonprofit organization in 1992.

28. Although the gender perspective posits that the social be analyzed with an understanding that "what is natural" for women and "what is natural" for men are social constructions, in some instances, it is conceptualized as the perspective that "includes" women. Whether in its broader or in its more restricted meaning, the gender perspective forces attention upon sexual difference and its symbolization and draws together many feminist demands.

29. It speaks volumes that the Vatican has come out against the term gender and has pressured for the elimination of this term from documents at both conferences. The Vatican did not achieve its goal.

30. The two members from the PRD, Amalia García and Rosario Robles, and one of the independent feminists, Patricia Mercado, are notable for their political interventions.

31. Lamas 1998a.
32. Ximena Bedregal's 1998 article offers a glimpse of the conflicts and practices of the women who call themselves autonomous.
33. The advertisement coordinated by GIRE on May 28, 1998, was signed by Octavio Paz, Elena Poniatowska, Carlos Fuentes, Carlos Monsiváis, and seventy other individuals.
34. The thirteen issues are the following: (1) public budgeting and the institutionalization of the focus on gender; (2) the right to a life free of violence; (3) social policies; (4) respect for sexual and reproductive rights; (5) political and civic participation; (6) commissions on equity and gender; (7) defending the secular state (*Estado Laíco*); (8) the right to nondiscrimination; (9) equitable distribution of family responsibilities; (10) strengthening federalism; (11) the right to free expression and information; (12) work, and (13) international commitments.
35. The secretaries of tourism, agrarian reform, and social development.
36. Sefchovich 2004.
37. Monárrez 2002.
38. Lamas, et al. 1995.
39. Monsiváis 1998.
40. Llamas and Rodríguez 1998.
41. GIRE 2004.
42. Barcellona 1996: 151.
43. Ibid.

2 Equal Opportunity and Affirmative Action in the Workplace

1. Walzer 1993: 10.
2. Ibid.
3. Scott 1992.
4. Dietz 1990.
5. Scott 1992.
6. Minow 1985.
7. Scott 1992.

8. Ibid.
9. Boccia 1990.
10. CINU 1966.
11. Bourdieu 1988.
12. Lamas 1989.

3 Gender: Some Conceptual and Theoretical Clarifications

1. Keynote speech at the Eighth Annual Colloquium on Gender Studies (*XIII Coloquio Anual de Estudios de Género*) of the University Program in Gender Studies at the UNAM, Mexico City, November 17, 2004.
2. Hawkesworth 1997.
3. Especially significant was the way the Vatican, a misogynist institution like few others, used its status as "observer" during UN conferences, especially those on Population and Development (Cairo, 1994) and on Women (Beijing, 1995) in order to pressure governments to eliminate the term *gender* from the text of the agreements. This attempt failed and the UN conferences legitimated the term in the international public sphere. Similarly to how the Vatican questioned the term *gender* and opposed its use, the archbishop and his representatives did the same in Mexico. There were symbolic rejections in spaces under Catholicism's overt influence: someone wrote a document in which it was argued that the term gender "offended Mexicans" and asked that it not be used in Mexico. See Lamas 2001.
4. Visweswaran 1997.
5. Hawkesworth 1997.
6. My examples are limited to a number of women writers in three anthropological communities: in Britain; France, and the United States, I do not include the Latin American community here because, even though the production of research about *gender* is substantial, it has not really been part of the theoretical debate. Nevertheless, I would like to mention two authors who explore the cases of anthropological studies of gender in our region: Gónzalez- Montes 1993 (beginning

with a panorama of the state of research), and Montecino 2002, who undertakes an analysis of the specificities and the obstacles to Latin American intellectual production and contrasts anthropologists from the South with those from the North.

7. This does not mean that the idea of gender was not already present in the thirties with Margaret Mead and that other anthropologists from the 1950s and 1960s would not use it later. Mary Goldsmith (1986) carefully reviews the debates that took place among Anglo-Saxon anthropologists regarding the studies of women and the appearance of the category of gender.

8. An example of this binary emphasis is the nearly simultaneous publication of two essays, one in the United States and another in France with nearly identical titles: "Is Female to Male as Nature Is to Culture?" by Sherry B. Ortner (1972), and "Man-Culture and Woman-Nature?" by Nicole-Claude Mathieu (1973). Ortner's work, revised and republished in the successful anthology by Rosaldo and Lamphere (1974), had a substantial influence on feminist thinking, and its structuralist position was questioned by Eleanor Leacock (1978, 1981), Karen Sacks (1982), and MacCormack and Strathern (1980). In 1996, Ortner looks at the contemporary relevance of this essay (173–180) and presents interesting nuances on the subject of the universality of masculine dominance and about her understanding of "structure:" in a Levi-Straussian sense, the search for broad regularities across time and space.

9. Yanagisako and Collier 1987; Strathern 1987.

10. As happens in a similar way in other disciplines, the alternate meaning of *gender* in English as sex and in Spanish as class, type, or species has lead to semantic and conceptual confusion about the way that this category is used. See Lamas 1996.

11. Rosaldo 1980: 390.

12. Rubin 1975.

13. The work of Helen Fisher has been particularly successful; in less than fifteen years (from 1983 to 1999), she was able to establish biological feminist evolutionism.

14. Spivak 1989.
15. Linda Alcoff is one of the theorists who have clearly explained the notion of "social positioning" in feminist theory. See Alcoff 1988.
16. Butler 1990.
17. Contrast Butler's formulation with that of Pierre Bourdieu on the *habitus* and how he uses it to look at the concept of reproduction. See Bourdieu 1991.
18. Moore 1988; ibid. 1994a; ibid. 1994b.
19. Although there were several factors preventing the adoption of Butler's theory, a fundamental one was the status of psychoanalysis in the social sciences in Europe. The use of psychoanalytic theory among French female social scientists also extended to the British, and a large number of women anthropologists had Lacanian backgrounds.
20. Butler 2004: 1.
21. The act of treating something as a fetish (*fetiche* in Spanish) means to have "exaggerated or irrational admiration" for (Dictionary of M. Moliner) and "excessive veneration" (Dictionary of the *Real Academia*) of something. A consequence of fetishization is the exclusion of that which does not resemble the fetish. This is the case with *Gender*, a book by Ivan Illich published in 1982 and translated into Spanish as *El género vernáculo* (1990). Reviewing the bibliographies of studies on *gender* in diverse disciplines—anthropology, sociology, history—the lack of references to Illich's book is notable. Why? Illich worked against the tendency to "forget" sexual difference. Although Illich was not able to translate his good intuitions clearly concerning the inescapable and foundational quality of sexual difference into writing, his dissident viewpoint provoked great hostility from US feminist academics, which meant that he was excluded from the most powerful circles of *gender* studies. This is an example of what Bourdieu and Wacquant (2001) have called the "ruses of imperialist reason," which operate, for example, by means of the imposition of research agendas—and bibliographies (!)—promoted by US *doxa* through its universities and foundations.

22. Schlegel 1990. Goldsmith finds that the debate between Leacock and Nash on ideology and practices is a fundamental antecedent to this delineation between general and specific meanings. Leacock 1981: 242–263.

23. Anne Fausto Sterling (1992 and 1993) insists that speaking of two sexes is not sufficient, since it does not include hermaphrodites and intersexed people with masculine or feminine tendencies (merms and ferms). Nevertheless, in the majority of societies, cultural blindness to these variations means that only two sexes are recognized.

24. Goldner 1991.

25. By referring to the immutable, Bourdieu (2000: 8) says that what appears to be eternal is solely the product of a project of eternalization carried out by (interconnected) institutions such as the family, the Church, the State, the school. The work of eternalizing is similar to that of naturalizing: it makes something constructed over the course of history by human beings appear to be "eternal" or "natural."

26. Dimen 1991.

27. Horigan, cited by Di Leonardo 1991: 30.

28. Goldsmith pointed out to me that many of the feminist anthropologists of the seventies were neoevolutionists, students of Service and Sahlins, and that there were also physical anthropologists, such as Leila Leibowitz and Jane Lancaster, who attempted to understand the relationship with the biological.

29. Three anthropological essays touch upon this subject: Roger Larsen 1979; Barbara Diane Miller 1993, and Marvin Harris 1993.

30. The work of feminist anthropologists in the field of assisted reproduction and new reproductive technologies is very interesting. See Héritier 1996, Strathern 1992, and Olavarría 2002.

31. This was one of the intentions behind the colloquium on "The Feminine Fact: What Is Being a Woman?" The presentations at this meeting were published in a book coordinated by Evelyne Sullerot, 1979. In addition, interesting pathways have been opened in evolutionary psychology, such as the works of Wright 1994 and Browne 2000.

32. Moore, 1999: 155.
33. Thus, despite the fact that human beings are distributed basically into two bodies (if we do not consider the intersexes mentioned by Fausto Sterling, 1993), there is a variety of combinations of identities and sexual orientations.
34. On this point, she is in agreement with Bourdieu, who argues in all of his writings for leaving behind the disastrous oppositions (such as established between the material and the ideal) that do not consider this complex interrelation.
35. Rosaldo 1980.
36. Bourdieu 1991.
37. See the Csordas' 1994 anthology, especially the introduction, in which she posits the body as representation and as way of being in the world. In addition, see the anthology of theoretical essays edited by Weiss and Haber 1999.
38. Roger Larsen explains: "Behavior is neither innate, nor acquired, but rather both of these at the same time" (1979: 352).
39. Moore 1999.
40. Scott 1986.
41. Ibid., 1999: 200.
42. Bourdieu 2000: 8.
43. Ibid.
44. Guelbenzu 2003.

4 Feminisms: Disagreements and Arguments

1. I appreciate the critical readings of Marisa Belausteguigoitia, Sandra Lorenzano, Araceli Mingo, Hortensia Moreno, Jorge Nieto-Montesinos, Mabel Piccini, María Teresa Priego, and Blanca Rico.
2. Hanssen 2000: 1.
3. Pereda 1999.
4. Ibid. 13.
5. Ibid.
6. Ibid. 14.
7. Ibid. 17.
8. Butler 1995.

9. Although I recognize the influence of feminist thinking in our countries (Lamas 2001), I am convinced that we need numerical growth in order to press forward politically.

10. I develop this concept more fully in "The Fetishization of Gender" ("*La fetichización del género*") in Lamas 2002.

11. Bourdieu and Wacquant 2001.

12. The quote is from an interview with Rooney. See Spivak 1989: 126.

13. By the way, I am critical of myself for not having made that distinction in my own criticism of *mujerismo* and *mujerista* positions.

14. Gallagher 1999: 55 (*Translation of quote by translator*).

15. For a quick review of the dangers of developing politics based on identity, see *Debate Feminista*, 1996 (No. 14), devoted to *Identities* [*Identidades*], in which Mouffe and Bondi follow their own lines of questioning.

16. Boccia 1990.

17. For the majority of "specialists" on gender, sexual difference is reduced to the anatomical differences of sex, and other singularities are not contemplated, neither of a biochemical nor psychic nature. The way that the unconscious is "forgotten" and the lack of knowledge about biomedical research, which has revealed that many physiological functions are influenced directly or indirectly by sex (Institute of Medicine 2001), are the underpinnings for constructivist mystification, which is so costly for the social sciences. The consequences of the psychic and the biological on human behavior must be included in any rigorous reflection on the distinct social status of women and men.

18. In her interview with Spivak, Ellen Rooney posits precisely this, that "context" is an antiessentialist concept (1989: 124).

19. Alcoff 1988.

20. Lauretis 1993.

21. It would appear that, in order to compensate for a lack of theorizations, our feminist academics have concentrated on the presentation of information from research or from archives. There is much work in sociology, with excellent

feminist researchers dealing with the female workforce and familial relationships in rural and urban contexts. In addition, their willingness to reread and reassess historical sources is noteworthy, since women's silence in the existing records is profound. This movement is beginning to gain strength in archeological work, that is, in the recovery of forgotten sites and silences of women authors that bear new information. This type of work is very fruitful, especially in literary historiography. Feminist researchers with a focus on women's discursive and life practices are beginning to be seen; feminist subjectivity is an object of research, as is political representation, specifically the repercussions of gender conflict on professional performance.

22. Amorós 1987.
23. See "From Protests to Proposals: Scenes from a Feminist Process" in this book. In addition, see the collective document "From Love to Necessity" [*"De amor a la necesidad"*] (Birgin et al. 1987).
24. Rancière 1996: 8.
25. Chantal Mouffe (1996) specifically addresses the distinction between antagonistic and agonistic.
26. I cannot help but think about the sad role of the French left in the 2000 elections. Incapable of forming a united front, they competed in the elections in a fragmented way. For this reason, they ended up with fewer votes than the far-right candidate and were forced, in the second round, to vote for the center-right candidate. We should be ready, because the same thing could happen to us.
27. Butler 1995.
28. We have accomplished too many good things together for us not to be able to dialogue with one another. We have made it possible for thousands of Latin American women to suffer less, and for other thousands, after questioning and changing their lives, to suffer in a different way. We have built organizations and networks, changed laws, transformed culture and politics. We have altered the domestic order. We have introduced a new perspective on the distinct relations

between the sexes, but we continue to be tied to rudimentary forms of rivalry and aggression with each another. Thus, despite the great deal we have accomplished in the outside world, having analyzed our internal relations in this essay, I speak of a "long night."

Bibliography

Acevedo, M., Del Valle, A., Lamas, M., Sánchez, M.E. and Zamarrón, G. "Piezas de un rompecabezas." *Fem* 5 (1978)

Acevedo, M., Lamas, M., and Liguori, A.L. 1980. "México: una bolsita de cal por las que van de arena." *Fem* 13, No. 2 (1978)

Aguilar Villanueva, Luis F. "¿ De quién es la política?" *Debate Feminista* 4 (1991)

Alcoff, Linda. "Poststructuralism and Cultural Feminism." *Signs* 13, No. 3 (1988)

Amorós, Celia. "Espacio de los iguales, espacio de las idénticas. Notas sobre poder y principio de individuación." *Arbor* (1987)

Amorós, Celia. *Feminismo, igualdad y diferencia*. Cuadernos del PUEG, 1995.

Barcellona, Pietro. *El individualismo propietario*. Ed. Trotta, 1996.

Bartra, Eli. et al. *La Revuelta*. Martín Casillas Editores, 1993.

Bartra, Eli, et al. *Feminismo en México, ayer y hoy*. Universidad Autónoma Metropolitana, 2002.

Bedregal, Ximena. "Ruptura de acuerdos de feministas autónomas." *Triple jornada* 3 (1998)

Beauvoir, Simone de. *El Segundo Sexo. Tomo II: La experiencia vivida*. Buenos Aires: Editorial Siglo XX, 1949.

Birgin, Haydée, et al. "Del amor a la necesidad." *Fem* 11, No. 60 (1987)

Birgin, Haydée. "Vivencias del encuentro de Chile: lo personal y lo político." *Debate Feminista* 15 (1997)

Bocchetti, Alessandra. "Para mí, para sí." *Debate Feminista* 2 (1990)

Bocchetti, Alessandra. *Lo que quiere una mujer*. Ediciones Cátedra, 1996.

Boccia, Maria Luisa. "Equívocos y diferencias de importancia." *Debate Feminista* 2 (1990)

Bondi, Liz. "Ubicar las políticas de la identidad." *Debate Feminista* 14 (1996)

Bourdieu, Pierre. "Social Space and Symbolic Power." *Sociological Theory* 7, No. 1 (1988)

Bourdieu, Pierre. *El sentido práctico.* Madrid: Ed. Taurus, 1991.

Bourdieu, Pierre. *La dominación masculina.* Barcelona: Anagrama, 2000.

Bourdieu, Pierre and Loïc J.D. Wacquant. *Las argucias de la razón imperialista.* Barcelona: Paidós, 2001.

Braunstein, Néstor. *Goce.* Mexico City: Siglo XXI Editores, 1990.

Brettell, Carolina B. and Carolyn F. Sargent. *Gender in Cross-Cultural Perspective.* Englewood Cliffs, NJ: Prentice Hall, 1993.

Browne, Kingsley R. *Biology at Work. Rethinking Sexual Equality.* New Brunswick, NJ: Rutgers University Press, 2000.

Butler, Judith. *Gender Trouble: Feminism and the Subversion of Identity.* New York: Routledge, 1990.

Butler, Judith. *El género en disputa. El feminismo y la subversión de la identidad.* Mexico City: Programa Universitario de Estudios de Género, UNAM, 2001.

Butler, Judith. *Bodies that Matter. On the Discursive Limits of "Sex."* New York: Routledge, 1993.

Butler, Judith. "For a Careful Reading." In *Feminist Contentions. A Philosophical Exchange,* eds. Seyla Benhabib, Judith Butler, Drucilla Cornell, Nancy Fraser, and Linda Nicholson. London: Routledge, 1995.

Butler, Judith. *Undoing Gender.* New York: Routledge, 2004.

Buxó Rey, María de Jesús. *Antropología de la Mujer.* Barcelona: Promoción Cultural, 1978.

Camou, Antonio. "Identidades a medida? (o de cómo entrar y salir de la modernidad por la puerta que más nos gusta)." *Debate Feminista* 14 (1996)

Cano, Gabriela. "Revolución, feminismo y ciudadanía en México (1915–1940)." In *Historia de las Mujeres. 5. El siglo XX,* eds. Georges Duby and Michelle Perrot. Madrid: Taurus, 1993.

Cano, Gabriela. "Las mujeres en el México del siglo XX. Una cronología mínima." In *Miradas feministas sobre las mexicanas del siglo XX*. Mexico City: Fondo de Cultura Económica, 2006.

Castellanos, Rosario. "La liberación de la Mujer, aquí." *Debate Feminista* 12 (1995)

Connell, Robert. "New Directions in Gender Theory, Masculinity Research and Gender Politics." *Ethnos* 61, No. 3–4 (1996)

Cos-Montiel, Francisco. "El traje nuevo de la emperatriz: lecciones de la integración de la perspectiva de género en México." *Debate Feminista* 28 (2003)

Cronin, Helena. *The Ant and the Peacock. Altruism and Sexual Selection from Darwin to Today*. Cambridge: Cambridge University Press, 1991.

Csordas, Thomas. "Introduction: The Body as Representation and Being in the World." In *Embodiment and Experience. The Existential Ground of Culture and Self*, ed. Thomas J. Csordas. Cambridge: Cambridge University Press, 1994.

Csordas, Thomas. "The Body's Career in Anthropology." In *Anthropological Theory Today*. Cambridge: Polity Press, 1999.

Chapa, María Elena. "Por qué el 30% mínimo de las oportunidades políticas para las mujeres." *Debate Feminista* 14 (1996)

Del Valle, Teresa. *Gendered Anthropology*. London: Routledge, 1993.

Del Valle, Teresa, ed. *Perspectivas feministas desde la antropología social*. Barcelona: Ariel Antropología, 2000.

Di Leonardo, Micaela. *Gender at the Crossroads of Knowledge. Feminist Anthropology in the Postmodern Era*. Berkeley: University of California Press, 1991.

Dietz, Mary G. "El contexto es lo que cuenta. Feminismo y teorías de la ciudadanía." In *Debate Feminista* 1 (1990)

Dimen, Muriel. "Deconstructing Difference: Gender, Splitting and Transitional Space." *Psychoanalytical Dialogue* 1 (1991)

Evans, Dylan. *Diccionario introductorio de psicoanálisis lacaniano*. Buenos Aires, Paidós, 1997.

EZLN. "Ley Revolucionaria de las Mujeres." In *Debate Feminista* 5, 9 (1994)

Fausto Sterling, Anne. *Myths of Gender. Biological Theories about Women and Men*. New York: Basic Books, 1992.

Fausto Sterling, Anne. "The Five Sexes. Why Male and Female are Not Enough." In *The Sciences*, 1993.

Ferrajoli, Luigi. *Derechos y garantías. La ley del más débil.* Madrid: Editorial Trotta, 1999.

Fisher, Helen E. *The Sex Contract. The Evolution of Human Behavior.* New York: Quill, 1983.

Fisher, Helen. *The First Sex.* New York: Random House, 1999.

Foucault, Michel. *Historia de la sexualidad: La voluntad del saber.* Mexico City: Siglo XXI Editores, 1977.

Foucault, Michel. *Historia de la sexualidad: El uso de los placeres.* Mexico City: Siglo XXI Editores, 1986.

Foucault, Michel. *Historia de la sexualidad: La inquietud de sí.* Mexico City: Siglo XXI Editores, 1987.

Frese, Pamela R. and John M. Coggeshall. *Transcending Boundaries. Multidisciplinary Approaches to the Study of Gender.* New York: Bergin and Garvey, 1991.

Freud, Sigmund. "Análisis terminable e interminable." In *Obras Completas, Tomo XXIII.* Buenos Aires: Amorrortu Editores, 1983.

Freud, Sigmund. *Fetichismo.* In *Obras completas. Tomo XXI.* Buenos Aires: Amorrortu Editores, 1983.

Freud, Sigmund. "El malestar en la cultura." In *Obras Completas, Tomo XXI.* Buenos Aires: Amorrortu Editores, 1983.

Freud, Sigmund. "La moral sexual 'cultural' y la nerviosidad moderna." In *Obras Completas, Tomo IX.* Buenos Aires: Amorrortu Editores, 1983.

Freud, Sigmund. "Sobre la más generalizada degradación de la vida amorosa.(Contribuciones a la psicología del amor II)." In *Obras completas, Tomo XI.* Buenos Aires: Amorrortu Editores, 1983.

Freud, Sigmund. "Sobre un tipo particular de elección de objeto en el hombre. (Contribuciones a la psicología del amor I)." In *Obras completas, Tomo XI.* Buenos Aires: Amorrortu Editores, 1983.

Freud, Sigmund. "Tres ensayos de teoría sexual." *Obras completas.* Buenos Aires: Amorrortu Editores, 1983.

Gallagher, Catherine. "El sujeto del feminismo o una historia del precedente." In *Retos de la postmodernidad. Ciencias Sociales y Humanas,* eds. Fernando J. García Selgas and José B. Monleón. Madrid: Editorial Trotta, 1999.

García, Amalia, Ifigenia Martínez and Nuria Fernández. "Las cuotas de las mujeres en el PRD: tres opiniones." *Debate Feminista*, 3 (1991)

Gargallo, Francesca. "El feo encuentro de la necesidad." *Debate Feminista* 15 (1997)

Gelb, Joyce. "Feminismo y acción política." In *Los nuevos movimientos sociales,* ed. Russell J. Dalton and Manfred Kuechler. Generalitat Valenciana: Alfons El Magnànim, 1992.

Giampino, Sylviane. *Les meres qui travaillent sont-elles coupables?.* Paris: Editions Albin Michel, 2000.

GIRE. *Paulina en el nombre de la ley.* Mexico City: GIRE (Temas para el debate, 2), 2000.

GIRE. *Paulina cinco años después.* Mexico City: GIRE (Temas para el debate, 4), 2004.

Goldner, Virginia. "Toward a Critical Relational Theory of Gender." *Psychoanalytical Dialogue* 1, 3 (1991)

Goldsmith, Mary. "Debates antropológicos en torno a los estudios sobre la mujer." In *Nueva Antropología* 7, 30 (1986)

Goldsmith, Mary. "Antropología de la mujer: ¿antropología de género o antropología feminista." *Debate Feminista* 3, 6 (1992)

González, María Cristina. *Autonomía y alianzas. El movimiento feminista en la ciudad de México 1976–1986.* Mexico City: UNAM-PUEG, 2001.

González Montes, Soledad. "Hacia una antropología de las relaciones de género en América Latina." In *Mujeres y relaciones de género en la antropología latinoamericana,* ed. Soledad González Montes. Mexico City: El Colegio de México, 1993.

González Rodríguez, Sergio. *Huesos en el desierto.* Mexico City: Anagrama, 2000.

Guelbenzu, José María. "Interview." *Babelia,* Supplement 631 in Newspaper El País. December 27, 2003.

Hawkesworth, Mary. "Confounding Gender." *Signs* 22, 3 (1997)

Hawkesworth, Mary. "Confundir el género." *Debate Feminista* 20 (1999)

Hanssen, Beatrice. *Critique of Violence. Between Postestructuralism and Critical Theory.* London: Routledge, 2000.

Harris, Marvin. "The Evolution of Human Gender Hierarchies: a Trial Formulation." In *Sex and Gender Hierarchies,* ed.

Barbara Diane Miller. Cambridge: Cambridge University Press, 1993.

Heritiér, Francoise. *Masculino/Femenino. El pensamiento de la diferencia*. Barcelona: Ariel, 1996.

Hirschman, Albert O. *Interés privado y acción pública*. Mexico City: Fondo de Cultura Económica, 1986.

Hirschman, Albert O. *Shifting Involvements. Private Interest and Public Action*. Princeton, NJ: Princeton University Press, 1982.

Horigan, Stephen. *Nature and Culture in Western Discourses*. London: Routledge and Kegan Paul, 1988.

Illich, Ivan. *Gender*. New York: Pantheon Books, 1982.

Illich, Ivan. *El género vernáculo*. Mexico City: Joaquín Mortiz Editores, 1990.

Institute of Medicine. *Exploring the Biological Contributions to Human Health: Does Sex Matter?* Washington, DC: National Academy Press, 2001.

Izquierdo, María Jesús. *El malestar en la desigualdad*. Madrid: Cátedra, 1998.

Jacoby, Russell. *La amnesia social*. Barcelona: Bosch Casa Editorial, 1984.

Jornadas Feministas. *Feminismo y sectores populares en América Latina, México D.F., noviembre de 1986*. Mexico City: EMAS, CIDHAI, GEM, MAS, CEM, COVAC, APIS, 1987.

Kuhn, Thomas. *La estructura de las revoluciones científicas*. Madrid: Alianza Editorial, 1989.

Lamas, Marta. "El movimiento de las costureras." In *Fem* 45 (1986)

Lamas, Marta. "Para romper un círculo vicioso: el valor comparable." In *Fuerza de trabajo femenina urbana en México. Participación económica y política,* eds. Jennifer Cooper, et al. Mexico City: UNAM-Coordinación de Humanidades/Miguel Ángel Porrúa, 1989.

Lamas, Marta. "El movimiento feminista en la década de los ochenta." In *Crisis y sujetos sociales en México*, ed. Enrique de la Garza Toledo. Mexico City: Centro de Investigaciones Interdisciplinarias en Humanidades-UNAM/Porrúa, 1992.

Lamas, Marta. "El movimiento feminista en México. Una interpretación." In *Mujeres y participación política: Avances y desafíos en*

América Latina, ed. Magdalena León. Bogotá: Tercer Mundo Editores, 1994.

Lamas, Marta. "Usos, dificultades y posibilidades de la categoría género." In *El género: la construcción cultural de la diferencia sexual*, ed. Marta Lamas. Mexico City: UNAM-PUEG/Porrúa, 1996.

Lamas, Marta. "De la A a la Z: A Feminist Alliance Experience." In *Women's Participation in Mexican Political Life*, ed. Victoria Rodríguez. Boulder: Westview Press, 1998.

Lamas, Marta. "Movimiento feminista y discurso político: los derechos sexuales y reproductivos en la construcción de una ciudadanía moderna." In *Avances en sexualidad y salud reproductiva*, ed. Juan Guillermo Figueroa and Claudio Stern. Mexico City: Colegio de México, 1998.

Lamas, Marta. "La radicalización democrática feminista." In *El reverso de la diferencia. Identidad y política*, ed. Benjamín Arditi. Caracas: Nueva Sociedad, 2000.

Lamas, Marta. *Política y reproducción. Aborto: la frontera del derecho a decidir*. Mexico City: Plaza y Janés, 2001.

Lamas, Marta. "Fragmentos de una autocrítica." In *Feminismo en México. Revisión histórico-crítica del siglo que termina*, ed. Griselda Gutiérrez Castañeda. Mexico City: Programa Universitario de Estudios de Género, UNAM, 2002.

Lamas, Marta. *Cuerpo: diferencia sexual y género*. Mexico City: Taurus, 2002.

Lamas, Marta, et al. "Encuentros y desencuentros: el Movimiento Amplio de Mujeres en México, 1970–1993." Mexico City: Ford Foundation, 1993.

Lamas Marta, et al. "Building bridges: the Growth of Popular Feminism in Mexico." In *The Challenge of Local Feminisms. Women's Movements in Global Perspective*, ed. Amrita Basu. Boulder, CO: Westview Press, 1995.

Lau Jaiven, Ana. *La nueva ola del feminismo en México*. Mexico City: Ed. Planeta, 1987.

Lauretis, Teresa de. "Upping the anti (sic) in feminist theory." In *The Cultural Studies Reader*, ed. Simon During. London: Routledge, 1993.

Leacock, Eleanor. "Women's Status in Egalitarian Society: Implications for Social Evolution." In *Current Anthropology* 33, 1978.

Leacock, Eleanor. *Myths of Male Dominance. Collected Articles on Women Cross-Culturally.* New York: Monthly Review Press, 1981.

Lees, Sue. "Aprender a amar. Reputación sexual, moral y control social de las jóvenes." In *Mujeres, derecho penal y criminología,* ed. Elena Larrauri. Madrid: Siglo Veintiuno de España Editores, 1994.

Leites, Edmund. *La invención de la mujer casta. La conciencia puritana y la sexualidad moderna.* Madrid: Siglo XXI, 1990.

Lepowsky, Maria. "Gender in an Egalitarian Society: A Case Study from the Coral Sea" in *Beyond the Second Sex. New Directions in the Anthropology of Gender,* eds. Sanday and Goodenough. Philadelphia: University of Pennsylvania Press, 1990.

Librería de Mujeres de Milán. *No creas tener derechos.* Madrid: Editorial Horas y Horas, 1991.

Lovera, Sara. "Magro fruto de la batalla por lograr una bancada feminista." *Debate Feminista* 4 (1991)

Llamas, Ma. Victoria and Claudia Rodríguez Ferrando. *Claudia. Una liberación.* Mexico City: Plaza y Janés, 1991.

Luhmann, Niklas. *El amor como pasión.* Barcelona: Ediciones Península, 1985.

Mascia-Lee, Frances, P. Sharpe, and C.B. Cohen. "The postmodernist turn in anthropology: cautions from a feminist perspective" *Signs* 15 (1989): 7–33.

Mascia-Lees, Frances and Nancy Johnson Black. *Gender and Anthropology.* Long Grove, IL: Waveland Press, 2000.

Massolo, Alejandra. *Por amor y coraje. Mujeres en movimientos urbanos de la ciudad de México.* Mexico City: El Colegio de México, 1992.

Mathieu, Nicole-Claude. "Homme-Culture et Femme- Nature?" *L'Homme* 13 (1973)

Mead, Margaret. *Growing up in New Guinea.* New York: Dell, 1968.

Mead, Margaret. *Macho y Hembra. Estudio de los sexos en un mundo en transición.* Caracas: Editorial Tiempo Nuevo, 1972.

Mead, Margaret. *Sexo y temperamento en las sociedades primitivas.* Barcelona: Editorial Laia, 1973.

Mercado, Patricia. "Lucha sindical y antidemocracia feminista." *Debate Feminista* 1 (1990).

Miller, Barbara Diane. "The Anthropology of Sex and Gender Hierarchies." In *Sex and Gender Hierarchies*, ed. Barbara Diane Miller, 3–31. Cambridge: Cambridge University Press, 1993.

Minow, Martha. "Learning to Live with the Dilemma of Difference: Bilingual and Special Education." *Law and Contemporary Problems* 2 (1984)

Moliner, María. *Diccionario de Uso del Español.* Madrid: Ed. Gredos, 1982.

Monárrez Fragoso, Julia. "Feminicidio sexual serial en Ciudad Juárez: 1993–2001." *Debate Feminista* 25 (2002).

Monsiváis, Carlos. Interview by author. Mexico City, November 29, 1998.

Monsiváis, Carlos. "El segundo sexo: no se nace feminista." *Debate Feminista* 20 (1999).

Montecino, Sonia. "Understanding Gender in Latin America." In *Gender's Place: Feminist Anthropologies of Latin America*, eds. Rosario Montoya, Lessie Jo Frazier and Janise Hurtig. New York: Palgrave Macmillan, 2002.

Montoya, Rosario, Lessie Jo Frazier, and Janise Hurtig. *Gender's Place. Feminist Anthropologies of Latin America.* New York: Palgrave Macmillan, 2002

Moore, Henrietta. *Feminism and Anthropology.* Cambridge: Polity Press, 1988.

Moore, Henrietta. *A Passion for Difference.* Cambridge: Polity Press, 1994.

Moore, Henrietta. "Gendered Persons: Dialogues between Anthropology and Psychoanalysis." In *Anthropology and Psychoanalysis: An Encounter through Culture*, eds. Suzette Heald and Ariane Deluz. London: Routledge, 1994.

Moore, Henrietta. "Whatever Happened to Women and Men?: Gender and Other Crises in Anthropology." In *Anthropological Theory Today*, ed. Henrietta Moore. Cambridge: Polity Press, 1999.

Mouffe, Chantal. "Feminismo, ciudadanía y política democrática radical." *Debate Feminista* 7 (1993)

Mouffe, Chantal. "Por una política de la identidad nómada." *Debate Feminista* 14 (1996)

Mutis, Alvaro. "La muerte del Estratega." In *La Mansión de Araucaima*. Buenos Aires: Sudamericana, 1973.

Nogués, Ramón M. *Sexo, cerebro y género. Diferencias y horizonte de igualdad*. Barcelona: Fundació Vidal i Barraquer/Paidos, 2003.

Offe, Claus. "Challenging the Boundaries of Institutional Politics: Social Movements Since the 1960's." In *Changing Boundaries of the Political*, ed. Charles S. Maier. Cambridge: Cambridge University Press, 1987.

Olavarría, María Eugenia. "De la casa al laboratorio. La teoría del parentesco hoy día." *Alteridades* 24 (2002): 99–116.

Ortner, Sherry. "Is Female to Male as Nature is to Culture?" *Feminist Studies* 2 (1972): 5–31.

Ortner, Sherry. "Is Female to Male as Nature is to Culture?" In *Women, Culture and Society*, eds. Rosaldo and Lamphere. California: Stanford University Press, 1974.

Ortner, Sherry. "Theory in Anthropology since the Sixties." *Comparative Studies in Society and History* 26 (1984): 126–166.

Ortner, Sherry. *Making Gender: The Politics and Erotics of Culture.* Boston, MA: Beacon Press, 1996.

Ortner, Sherry and Harriet Whitehead. *Sexual Meanings: the Cultural Construction of Gender and Sexuality*. Cambridge: Cambridge University Press, 1981.

Pasternak, Burton, Carol R. Ember, and Melvin Ember. *Sex, Gender and Kinship: A Cross Cultural Perspective*. Englewood Cliffs, NJ: Prentice Hall, 1997.

Pateman, C. *The Sexual Contract*. Cambridge: Polity Press, 1988.

Pereda, Carlos. *Crítica de la razón arrogante*. Mexico City: Taurus, 1999.

Rancière, Jacques. *El desacuerdo. Política y filosofía*. Buenos Aires: Ediciones Nueva Visión, 1996.

Ramoneda, Josep. *El sentido íntimo*. Barcelona: Muchnick Editores, 1982.

Randolph, Richard R., David M. Schneider, and May N. Díaz. *Dialectics and Gender. Anthropological Approaches*. Boulder, CO: Westview Press, 1988.

Reiter, Rayna R., ed. *Toward an Anthropology of Women.* New York/ London: Monthly Review Press, 1975.

Ricoeur, Paul. "Psicoanálisis y cultura." In *Sociología contra psicoanálisis.* Barcelona: Ediciones Martínez Roca, 1974.

Rodríguez, Victoria. *Women's Participation in Mexican Political Life.* Boulder, CO: Westview Press, 1998.

Rosaldo, Michelle and L. Lamphere, eds. *Women, Culture and Society.* California: Stanford University Press, 1974.

Rosaldo, Michelle."The Use and Abuse of Anthropology: Reflections on Feminism and Cross-Cultural Understanding." *Signs* 5 (1980): 389–417.

Rubin, Gayle. "The Traffic in Women: Notes on the 'Political Economy' of Sex." In *Toward an Anthropology of Women*, ed. Rayna R. Reiter. New York: Monthly Review Press, 1975.

Sacks, Karen. *Sisters and Wives: The Past and Future of Sexual Equality.* Chicago, IL: University of Illinois Press, 1982.

Sanday, Peggy. *Female Power and Male Dominance.* Cambridge: Cambridge University Press, 1981.

Sanday, Peggy Reeves and Ruth Gallagher Goodenough, ed. *Beyond the Second Sex: New Directions in the Anthropology of Gender.* Philadelphia, PA: University of Pennsylvania Press, 1990.

Saraceno, Chiara. "Diferencia sexual: jaula o atajo." *Debate Feminista* 2 (1990)

Sartre, Jean Paul. *L'existencialisme est un humanisme.* Paris: Nagel, 1946.

Savater, Fernando. *Ética como amor propio.* Madrid: Mondadori, 1988.

Schlegel, Alice. "Sexual Antagonism in a Sexually Egalitarian Society." *Ethos* 7 (1979): 124–141.

Schlegel, Alice. "Gender Meanings: General and Specific." *Beyond the Second Sex: New Directions in the Anthropology of Gender*, eds. Peggy Reeves Sanday and Ruth Gallagher Goodenough. Philadelphia, PA: University of Pennsylvania Press, 1990.

Scott, Joan W. "Gender: A Useful Category of Historical Analysis." *American Historical Review* 91 (1986): 1053–1075.

Scott, Joan W.. "Los usos de la teoría." *Debate Feminista* 5 (1992)

Scott, Joan W. "El género: una categoría útil para el análisis histórico." In *El género: la construcción cultural de la diferencia sexual*, ed. Marta Lamas. Mexico City: UNAM-PUEG/Porrúa, 1996.

Scott, Joan W. "Some More Reflections on Gender and Politics." In *Gender and the Politics of History*, ed. Joan. W. Scott. New York: Columbia University Press, 1999.

Sefchovich, Sara. *Veinte preguntas ciudadanas a la mitad más visible de la pareja presidencial*. Mexico City: Océano, 2004.

Slater, Philip. *The Pursuit of Loneliness*. Boston, MA: Beacon Press, 1970.

Spivak, Gayatri Chakravorty. "In a Word." Interview with Ellen Rooney. *Differences* 2 (1989)

Strathern, Marilyn. "No Nature, No Culture: the Hagen Case." In *Nature, Culture and Gender*, eds. C. MacCormack and M. Strathern. Cambridge: Cambridge University Press, 1980.

Strathern, Marilyn. "Dual models and Multiple Persons: Gender in Melanesia." 85th Annual Meeting of the American Anthropological Association. Philadelphia, November 1986.

Strathern, Marilyn. "An Awkward Relationship: the Case of Feminism and Anthropology." *Signs* 12 (1987): 276–292.

Strathern, Marilyn. *The Gender of the Gift*. Berkeley: University of California Press, 1988.

Strathern, Marilyn. *Reproducing the Future: Anthropology, Kinship and the New Reproductive Technologies*. Manchester: Manchester University Press, 1992.

Strathern, Marilyn. *Shifting Contexts: Transformations in Anthropological Knowledge*. London: Routledge, 1995.

Sullerot, Evelyne, ed. *El hecho femenino.¿Qué es ser mujer?.* Barcelona: Editorial Argos Vergara, 1979.

Tannen, Deborah. *Gender and Discourse*. Oxford: Oxford University Press, 1994.

Tarrés, Maria Luisa. "Hacia un equilibrio de la ética y la negociación." *Debate Feminista* 7 (1993)

Tarrés, Maria Luisa. "Discurso feminista y movimiento de mujeres en México (1970–2000)." In *Miradas feministas sobre las mexicanas del siglo XX*. Mexico City: FCE, 2006.

Tuñón, Esperanza. *Mujeres en escena: de la tramoya al protagonismo (1982–1994)*. Mexico City: Miguel Angel Porrúa/UNAM-PUEG/Ecosur, 1997

VII Encuentro Nacional Feminista. "Feminismo, vida cotidiana y política: una propuesta de acción afirmativa." *Debate Feminista* 7 (1993)

Visweswaran, Kamala. *Fictions of Feminist Ethnography.* Minneapolis: University of Minnesota Press, 1994.

Visweswaran, Kamala. "Histories of Feminist Ethnography." In *Annual Review of Anthropology* 26 (1997): 591–621.

Walzer, Michel. *Spheres of Justice: A Defense of Pluralism and Equality.* New York: Basic Books, 1983.

Walzer, Michel. *Las esferas de la justicia.* Mexico City: FCE, 1993.

Weiss, Gail and Honi Fern Haber. *Perspectives on Embodiment: The Intersections of Nature and Culture.* London: Routledge, 1999.

Welldon, Estela. *Madre, virgen, puta. Idealización y deningración de la maternidad.* Madrid: Siglo XXI, 1993.

Wright, Robert. *The Moral Animal. Evolutionary Psychology and Everyday Life.* New York: Vintage Books, 1994.

Yanagisako, Sylvia and Jane Collier. "Toward a Unified Analysis of Gender and Kinship." In *Gender and Kinship: Essays Towards an Unified Analysis*, eds. Sylvia Yanagisako and Jane Collier. Stanford: Stanford University Press, 1987.

Index

CPSIA information can be obtained at www.ICGtesting.com
Printed in the USA
LVOW101206290612

288179LV00003B/11/P